T0255786

AI FOR SCHOOL TEACHERS

AI FOR EVERYTHING

Artificial Intelligence (AI) is all around us. From driverless cars to game-winning computers to fraud protection, AI is already involved in many aspects of life, and its impact will only continue to grow in the future. Many of the world's most valuable companies are investing heavily in AI research and development, and not a day goes by without news of cutting-edge breakthroughs in AI and robotics.

The AI for Everything series will explore the role of AI in contemporary life, from cars and aircraft to medicine, education, fashion, and beyond. Concise and accessible, each book is written by an expert in the field and will bring the study and reality of AI to a broad readership including interested professionals, students, researchers, and lay readers.

For more information about this series please visit:
https://www.routledge.com/AI-for-Everything/book-series/AIFE

AI FOR SCHOOL TEACHERS

Rose Luckin
Karine George
Mutlu Cukurova

CRC Press
Taylor & Francis Group
Boca Raton London New York

CRC Press is an imprint of the
Taylor & Francis Group, an **informa** business

CRC Press
Boca Raton and London

First Edition published 2022
by CRC Press
6000 Broken Sound Parkway NW, Suite 300, Boca Raton, FL 33487-2742

and by CRC Press
4 Park Square, Milton Park, Abingdon, Oxon, OX14 4RN

CRC Press is an imprint of Taylor & Francis Group, LLC

Library of Congress Cataloging-in-Publication Data

Names: Luckin, Rosemary, author. | George, Karine, author. | Cukurova, Mutlu, author.
Title: AI for school teachers / Rose Luckin, Karine George, Mutlu Cukurova.
Description: First edition. | Boca Raton : CRC Press, 2022. | Series: AI for everything | Includes bibliographical references and index.
Identifiers: LCCN 2021045710 | ISBN 9781032044354 (hardback) | ISBN 9781032037714 (paperback) | ISBN 9781003193173 (ebook)
Subjects: LCSH: Educational technology. | Artificial intelligence. | Education--Effect of technological innovations on. | Computer-assisted instruction.
Classification: LCC LB1028.3 .L82 2022 | DDC 371.33--dc23/eng/20211109
LC record available at https://lccn.loc.gov/2021045710

ISBN: 978-1-032-04435-4 (hbk)
ISBN: 978-1-032-03771-4 (pbk)
ISBN: 978-1-003-19317-3 (ebk)

DOI: 10.1201/9781003193173

Typeset in Joanna
by Deanta Global Publishing Services, Chennai, India

CONTENTS

FOREWORD

We are all using products powered by Artificial Intelligence (AI) every day, whether we're searching for the route with the least traffic, translating foreign language websites, or playing our favourite songs using voice commands. But AI technologies go far beyond making life more convenient; its development makes breakthroughs in seemingly Herculean tasks like folding proteins to better understand the human body to optimising data centres and sequestering carbon to meet net-zero emissions. The achievement of these innovations hinges on AI technologies being built responsibly – slowly, safely, securely, and in the public interest.

There are risks to this technology, as well as rewards: risks which need to be regulated and risks which the industry must mitigate and ultimately root out. Governments and businesses typically need public pressure in order to act and when it comes to technology, citizens aren't yet shouting from the rooftops for change.

The public's relationship with AI technology is complicated. This is understandable as the sector can feel opaque, perceived as a "tech bro's" domain, driven by the 1% and rushing at an unbearably fast pace.

On the one hand, the public are given vague promises of social benefit. Starting simply, it will recognize your face and unlock your phone; it will help you find the perfect movie. Escalating further, it will do the dirty, dangerous, dull jobs you don't want to; it will also drive your car and look after your pets. This can lead to people picking convenience over privacy – citizens accepting the immediate benefits and not questioning the impacts, not taking a breath to ask why. Who was this made for? What do I unwittingly give up when I use these technologies? What is that worth? And then moments like the 2020 A-Level grading fiasco occur and we have students screaming "f**k the algorithm" outside 10 Downing Street. Regardless of the fact that experts on the matter believe this to be a case of basic maths (not AI) used inappropriately, asking the wrong question in a setting it had no place being, the press and the public saw this as a mutant AI algorithm causing a whole cohort, and maybe generation, to be disadvantaged.

The consequence? At best – public scepticism about AI. At worst – a rejection of its potential for good entirely.

Too many people are getting left behind. The digital divide is widening with increased inequality and the AI ecosystem is failing to inspire or earn the trust of the public. This new technology feels inaccessible or is inaccessible. It's believed to be overhyped or unclear and ultimately people end up believing that it isn't for them.

In order for AI to bring around benefits for society and the economy, everyone needs to be involved in some way. Whether that's building, living with, working with or playing with this technology, it's now clear, everyone needs to have basic AI and Data Literacy to consciously engage safely.

As chair of the UK Government AI Council, I've made it my mission to encourage the progress of AI to be made in lockstep with the public. I believe the ecosystem should engage the public, listen, and act based on their views.

In June 2020, the AI Council agreed we needed to set out our collective vision for how AI should develop in the UK. One of the key pillars was dedicated to skills and diversity. We suggested the government double down on initiatives to grow, welcome and retain the best AI research and engineering talent in the UK. Alongside this we highlighted the need to ensure the workforce is ready for an AI-enabled future and that the nation feels prepared for a life permeated by this technology.

So how will we inspire people to careers in AI – in the UK and worldwide? How will we help people learn how to learn and work ethically and effectively alongside smarter digital tools driven by AI? Public campaigns will surely play a part, but education – school-age education, national curriculums, and initiatives for lifelong learning – will be critical channels for this engagement.

That is why this book, by Rose Luckin, Karine George, and Mutlu Cukurova, all talented and accomplished educators in their own right, is so very timely and so well focused. Focusing on teachers, the front line, those with the toughest jobs, those preparing people to build and operate in our increasingly AI-supported societies is invaluable.

Up until now, teachers have been in a position similar to the majority of the general public. AI was a "too busy to bother" area that they did not understand or particularly trust, and given competing priorities, they did not feel great pressure to understand. But with education technologies being thrust front and centre during the pandemic, there has been a shift. AI is now increasingly seen as a valuable tool for teaching and learning, and a critical component of the knowledge people will need to flourish. The pressure for teachers to understand and shape this new arena has well and truly arrived.

With this volume, Rose, Karine, and Mutlu have written an accessible, very human, handbook to help any teacher become "AI-ready". After a brief review of the definitions, origins, and history of AI, they swiftly dive into the practicalities of why and how a teacher might engage with AI technologies in their teaching practice. Useful guiding questions and frameworks are interspersed with examples and explanations drawn from schools and the learning sciences. Advice on the smart and ethical collection of data is also included, to help teachers more easily surface evidence to that seemingly elusive question of what will work in their classrooms for their students, in keeping with the learning outcomes they hope to achieve.

Importantly, the authors assure us we don't need to be experts or data scientists to be substantively engaged with AI, which is a relief as I myself am not and, indeed, most people won't be. And this is pointedly not a book solely for STEM teachers – the influence of AI will touch teaching and learning tools across the piste, and the implications of its use have bearing across all subjects whether it be English, maths, geography, or philosophy. What is needed is a *general understanding* of the ingredients that comprise AI, and the ways we are able to combine them for the realisation of human potential. It's this general understanding that unlocks the gateway to the AI debate. And with this book, Rose, Karine, and Mutlu have provided teachers an all-access pass to one of the most important public conversations of our era. Jump right in, enjoy the ride, and then take everyone on it with you!

Tabitha Goldstaub
London, UK
August 2021

INTRODUCTION: UNDERSTANDING THE INGREDIENTS

In the firm belief that an introduction to the authors is an important complement to an introduction to the book that they have written, we begin with a bit about ourselves.

I am Rose and I love Artificial Intelligence (AI), but I love people more. I imagine that you already love people – well, some people at least – but perhaps not AI. I hope that when you reach the end of this short book, you will at least feel that you have made friends with AI.

Love takes a little longer.

A TALE OF LOVE AND LEARNING TO START OUR STORY ABOUT AI

When I was a small girl I loved spending time with my grandfather in his garden, he had been a market gardener all his working life, and whilst now retired, he still had an amazing garden. It was the sort of garden that you could imagine Peter Rabbit[1] and his pals bounding about in and having fun.

There were two green houses, one for tomatoes and the other for cucumbers, plus just a few glasshouse strawberries, so that he could be sure there would be a punnet of glorious, jewel-like Royal Sovereign berries popping with sweet flavour, just waiting to burst out on my tongue and leave me with scarlet juice running down my chin when my birthday came along in June.

Throughout most of the rest of the garden, there were neat rows where flourished potatoes, and peas, carrots and onions, soft fruits and berries, plus a few rows of flowers to be cut for the house and for friends. He tended them daily until the day he died, with care and attention, and a little love too, I am sure.

I adored helping him with the hoe, planting seedlings and feeling the earth between my fingers or deadheading the flowers. He even showed me how to prune the roses, although I was not actually allowed to use the secateurs until I was quite a lot older. But, most of all I loved taking out the side shoots from the tomato plants in the greenhouse, because the smell was simply divine. The greenhouse was whitewashed, and, in addition to a range of tomato plants organised in carefully tied trusses, it also contained French marigolds to keep away the black and white fly. The smell was hot, spicy, musky, and tangy, the air tasted of the plump fruit that the plants would bear, with a hint of citrus and pepper from the marigolds. To this day, the smell of a hot tomato glasshouse, or a bed of marigolds on a sunny day, immediately evokes strong emotions and memories for me.

This may sound idyllic, and I believe that it was, but I was not an angelic or perfect gardener who always worked hard. I also liked to play of course and my grandfather created a swing for me by looping a rope over a big branch of the plum tree that provided welcome shade for the small lawn. I would swing and play imaginary games, daydreaming the afternoon away. I would also spend many hours simply watching my grandfather as he worked away.

I learned so much in so many ways; I was shown, trained, practised, and I watched and watched the expert as he toiled away happily. I loved him, I loved his garden, and I loved the way that he set me up for life to love nature, plants, nurturing growth, and watching things develop and transform themselves with the changing seasons each year.

AI is clever, but it can only scratch the surface of the learning experience that I describe here. As you read on, you will discover the way in which AI gains its expertise and learns from experience. You will *not* find anything at all about how it smells, tastes, hoes, deadheads, experiences the breeze as a swing moves through the air, feels love, or the warmth of the earth, or wonder at the memories that have shaped its mind. Never forget that human intelligence is amazing and far richer than anything even the canniest computer can muster.

THE NOT-A-'DIGITAL NINJA' HEADTEACHER

For me (Karine), as a co-author of this book and a headteacher for more than 20 years in state-funded schools, understanding AI was a pathway to seizing back the reins of a curriculum that had become overly prescriptive and rigid. In AI I saw the promise of mechanisms to alleviate the burden of iterative, preparation, administrative, evaluation, and feedback tasks so that teachers could reconnect with young people to support and enhance their learning in more meaningful ways. And now, with the benefit of more experience, I see AI as the enabler that will allow every school, in its own unique context, to develop a strategy that will improve the educational opportunities for each student in new and exciting ways with evidence-informed practice.

At this point, you may be thinking that I must be one of those rare digital ninja headteachers. This could not be further from reality. In fact, when I first discussed the development of a technology strategy with the staff of my school, they fell about laughing, which perhaps gives you a sense of my relative level of expertise. But no matter: I went into teaching, and then headship to make a difference to the life chances of the children in my care and to support them to be *life-ready*, *work-ready*, and *world-ready*. Collectively, as educators, we know that technology, in all its forms, is clearly going to play an influential part in that.

With each passing day, we see how the advances humans are making in AI are changing our world. Perhaps most importantly, these advances are transforming the world of work. This transformation has significant implications for all of us. As long-time educators, we are particularly concerned about the implications for teachers. Teachers are responsible in large part for preparing students to act wisely and well – now, and in the future. Increasingly this demands that teachers have a working understanding of AI, so that they can do two things:

1   Use AI safely and effectively to support their students' learning
2   Help students understand how AI works and how to use the power it brings ethically

We have joined forces to co-author this book, because we want you to see the ways in which AI can help you, and we want you to understand how to work alongside AI, so that it augments what you are able to achieve as a teacher, school leader, parent, school governor, or trustee. But most of all we want you to realise how amazing your own human intelligence and brain power is, so that you can keep AI firmly in its place: a tool to make you and those around you smarter.

The aim of this book is, therefore, to help teachers understand enough about AI to buy tools that will be useful and appropriate to their context, to use AI effectively, and to help other people to do the same. (Note we say "understand enough" because a person does not need to be an AI expert nor a data scientist to be AI-savvy. More on this later.) We use educational examples throughout to illustrate our points. We have already laid out why *we* think it is critical for teachers to understand AI.

* * *

A good place to start our discussion on understanding AI is with the AIs you are already using. For example, many people use speech to text when they dictate a note on their mobile phone. The software that turns the sound made by their voice into the words and spaces that appear in the note is a form of AI. Similarly, you might be using a voice-activated personal assistant in your home or on your phone. Siri, Alexa, and Google Home are all examples of this kind of device. In this example, the AI analyses the sounds that come in through the microphone, interprets the meaning of these sounds, constructs a response, and expresses the response as spoken words.

Of course, there are many, many ways in which AI is being used by billions of people across the world. From Google searches to online shopping and phone apps that help you navigate the world, AI is being used all the time. And it is already being used in schools. For example, there are adaptive platforms that help students on an individual basis through an AI that adjusts the tasks the student is asked to complete and the amount of help they are given. We provide some examples of these systems in the endnotes to this chapter.

When anybody decides to spend money on AI they should understand what the AI is doing and what the AI can do. This does not mean that they need to understand how to build an AI system or to write computer code. It just means that they need a *general understanding* of what is happening inside the "black box" of AI.

Let's use an analogy to get at what we mean by a general understanding. A child would like to make cupcakes for their school friends. Their elder sister, who hates to bake, offers to help by going to the shop. The sister does not need to know precisely *how* to make cupcakes to help. She does, however, need to know that cupcakes require a set of ingredients that will be mixed and baked, and that she can find the ingredients in a recipe book. It would also be useful for her to know that without the correct ingredients, the cupcakes will not be successful and that she can find out more from the recipe book if a parent is not home in time to oversee the eventual mixing and baking of the cupcakes.

The general AI understanding we are aiming to help you gain in this book is akin to the understanding required by the sister in this cupcake analogy. To have a general understanding of baking, you will need to know that you need ingredients, a method for combining the ingredients, a way to cook those mixed ingredients, a sense of what the result of a specific set of ingredients is likely to look and taste like, and an understanding whether the result (cupcakes) is *actually the right one for you*. One would hope our fictional sister would know that the purchasing of the ingredients, the mixing, and the baking involved in cupcake making should not be used if what she really wants to produce is a classic English breakfast! For teachers, just as with our big sister, it is important to know what we are trying to make – what are the educational outcomes we hope to achieve for our students and school with the help of AI.

There is an increasing array of different technologies out there to be bought and used in teaching and learning. And whilst it is impossible to fully know the ever-changing universe of AI products and services, it is entirely possible to know the basic types of ingredients and processing that will be driving different sorts of AI technology. Each chapter in this book is designed to help you to understand those ingredients, so that you will begin to know the right questions to ask of technology vendors when and if you decide to bring a new tool into your school.

The seven chapters of this book are framed around the steps of the AI Readiness Framework, a framework developed in collaboration with our colleagues at Educate Ventures[2] (Figure I.1).

In the first chapter, we will introduce you to AI and take you through the first step in the AI Readiness Framework. We will discuss what AI is and how you can develop an AI mindset. In particular, we will explain why data is so important to modern machine learning AI. Chapter 2 will take you through Step 2 of the framework to explore the types of challenges faced by school leaders and teachers today. We provide a set of criteria that can be used by you to select one to three challenges that can become the

The 7 steps to AI Readiness: EThICAL

There are seven key steps to getting you and your organisation ready to leverage the transformational power of AI. These can be found in the 'EThICAL AI Readiness' framework:

1) **Educate, enthuse, excite** – people about building an AI mindset within your community

2) **Tailor and hone** - the particular challenges you want to focus on

3) **Identify** – identify (wisely), access and collate data that has already been collected

4) **Collect** – new data relevant to your focused challenge

5) **Apply** – prepare your data and apply AI techniques

6) **Learn** – understand what the data is telling you about your focus

7) **Iterate** - return to step 1 (or any other previous step) and work through until you are condiment that you are AI ready

And all these steps should be done ethically

Figure I.1   The 7 steps to AI Readiness.

focus for AI Readiness. Data is at the centre of Chapter 3, as we tackle Step 3 to explore the sources of data that might be available to help us understand more about the sorts of challenges that we face in education. Chapter 4 explores what new data could be collected to help us understand more about our challenges and we complete Step 4. In Chapter 5 and Step 5, we illustrate how AI can be applied to the sorts of data that educators can access to learn about the challenges we face. Chapter 6 investigates the sorts of information that AI can help us to extract from the data we have collected about a challenge that we have identified. This completes Step 6. Finally, Chapter 7 looks at how AI Readiness can be used to understand AI-driven products and services available to schools. We also return to the question of ethics and provide practical guidance to help you make the right decisions about trying and buying AI for your school.

Throughout this book, we contextualise the way we talk about AI within a school setting. We hope that this will make the explanations that we provide more accessible and interesting. We also hope that it will make you want to encourage your peers and colleagues to want to know more about AI too. You will also find resources for related further reading at the end of each chapter.

We hope you enjoy reading this book, that you find it useful, and that at the end you will feel able to choose and use the best AI for you and your students.

NOTES

1 Potter, B. (2002). *The Tale of Peter Rabbit*. London: Frederick Warne.
2 https://www.educateventures.com. In particular, Dr Carmel Kent, Dr Mutlu Cukurova, and Prof Benedict du Boulay.

1

WHAT IS AI AND WHY MIGHT AI BE USEFUL IN EDUCATION?

How can AI benefit education? What is AI and how can I use it effectively? What sort of AI do I need? These might be some of the questions you are asking yourself. Before we dive into these questions, let's take a moment to get clear on *what* AI is and *why* AI might be useful. We will also try to enthuse you about AI's potential for use in education.

WHAT IS AI?

The term "Artificial Intelligence", abbreviated to AI, is not something for which there is any single accepted definition. Many scientists disagree about exactly what the precise definition of AI should include. As this chapter will explain, there are two main types of AI: machine learning and Good Old-Fashioned AI (GOFAI). Some people believe that only machine learning should be called AI, but many others believe that the definition of AI should also include tools and technologies that make intelligent decisions in other ways. We have selected a simple definition of AI in an attempt to include the vast array of different sorts of tools and technologies that could be considered to come within the bounds of the phrase "Artificial

DOI: 10.1201/9781003193173-1

Intelligence". The definition we have selected is taken from the *Oxford English Dictionary*:[1]

> The capacity of computers or other machines to exhibit or simulate intelligent behaviour.

A SHORT HISTORY OF AI

MACHINES THAT COULD BEHAVE, BUT NOT INTELLIGENTLY

With a definition in place, let's look back at where AI has come from. For many centuries, humans have been intrigued by the task of creating representations of living creatures, including humans. These representations are often referred to as automata and they date back to the Middle Ages, possibly even earlier. In the 19th and early 20th centuries, automata reached the height of their popularity. From bears that could turn somersaults to magicians who could see another automata in half, and nightingales that sang in golden cages, these party pieces were increasingly intricate and could perhaps be considered forerunners of AI.

Or perhaps more accurately, we might consider them to be the forerunners of the field of cybernetics, which is a scientific area of study that explores the control and communication that happens in animals and in machines. The study of cybernetics was started by Norbert Viner in the mid-20th century and is still very much at the heart of what robots can do. These cybernetic robot predecessors were more mechanical than intelligent, but their creation influenced the field of robotics that evolved. Even today, not all robots are intelligent; some are just labour saving through their speedy completion of mechanical, repetitive tasks. However, many robots are also intelligent and are part of the human desire, played out over time, to create objects that can behave in intelligent ways.

We also love to tell stories about objects that behave intelligently, and robots have long been a love of the film-making industry. Who cannot but be endeared by robot characters like *Star Wars*' C-3PO,[2] or WALL-E,[3] feel fearful of *Blade Runner's* Roy Batty[4] or The Borg,[5] and simply be amazed by Ava in *Ex Machina!*[6] The reality is nothing so dramatic. It is certainly true that intelligent software and robots are a reality, but none of them have the all-round capabilities of their movie-star peers. The ability of AI systems to achieve more than one area of expertise is still mainly a fantasy. From tangible robots to invisible software, AI is a specialist operator with no ability to transition from one area of expertise to another. A self-driving car cannot play chess; a surgical robot cannot drive a car. It's worth noting, however, that a human surgeon can likely drive a car and play chess and a great deal more besides.

But let us return to our brief look back at the history of AI.

Another important person in the history of AI is Alan Turing who, in 1950, wrote a famous article titled "Computing machinery and intelligence" in which he posed the question: "Can machines think?"[7] Alan Turing was a mathematician and code breaker at Bletchley Park during the Second World War. Turing proposed a clever test that could be used to decide if a machine was thinking and, therefore, was intelligent. This test, which is called the Turing Test, presents the proposition that if a computer can fool a human into believing that it is really a human, then that machine deserves to be called intelligent. This thought experiment captured the interest of many scientists and helped to progress the birth of AI. Indeed, there are still Turing Test challenges today in which computer scientists pit their AI against one another to see whose system can convince the most people.

THE TEN MEN WHO GAVE BIRTH TO MODERN AI

Following the publication of Turing's famous article, the field of AI evolved at a rapid pace, and in 1956 a momentous meeting took place at Dartmouth College in New Hampshire, in the United States.[8] A ten-man group of scientists met with the aim of studying human intelligence in all its richness and from all aspects. Their goal was to be able to describe each feature of human intelligence so precisely that a machine could be built to simulate it. The scientists believed that they would be able to make significant advances towards their goal over the period of a summer.

They soon discovered that human intelligence was far more complicated than they had understood and progress during that summer was small. Nonetheless, the occasion of this meeting was extraordinarily significant, as it gave birth to what we now recognise as the scientific discipline of AI.

It is interesting to wonder had the ten scientists been from more diverse backgrounds, if their group would have taken AI in a different direction. We will never know. What we can be sure about is that the lack of diversity amongst those who work in AI is an ever-present concern. We hope that by making AI accessible to more people, a more diverse population might become interested in working with AI.

From that date onwards, the task of creating computer programs that behaved in intelligent ways was the cutting edge of science. At this stage, AI was not focused on robotics, but on developing software that could enable computers to interact intelligently. Early attempts were very simple. Systems such as ELIZA,[9] a computer program that played the role of a psychotherapist, were text-based and required the person playing the role of the patient to type out their problems and questions. The ELIZA software was programmed to look for keywords in what the patient typed. When a keyword or phrase was found, the software triggered a stock answer template and ELIZA offered her advice in the text on the computer screen. It is hard to believe that anything so crude could fool anyone into consulting with ELIZA for more than an initial sentence. But several people were duped by ELIZA, at least for a while.

GOOD OLD-FASHIONED AI AND EXPERT SYSTEMS

If those ten scientists who met in New Hampshire are considered the fathers of AI, then maybe ELIZA should be the mother.[10] The important thing about systems like ELIZA is that it identified a particular approach to simulating intelligent behaviour. This approach is called production rule-based pattern matching and ELIZA "gave birth" to many similar systems over the decades following her inception in 1964. In fact, the production rule-based systems that evolved from ELIZA became sophisticated enough to accomplish advanced activities such as diagnosing an illness from a set of symptoms and suggesting the treatment regime based on these symptoms. These systems are referred to as expert systems and were used in a variety of different fields, such as medicine.

The pinnacle of the GOFAI movement came in 1997 when a system built by IBM, called Deep Blue,[11] beat the then chess grandmaster Gary Kasparov at the game of chess. This was extremely impressive and marked the high point of this phase in AI's history.

The problem with these Good Old-Fashioned AI (GOFAI) systems was that the actions the AI was able to perform had to be pre-programmed into the software when it was written – a huge task. For games like chess, there may only be a certain number of moves that each particular chess piece can take, but there are many millions of iterations that the combination of these moving chess pieces can create. In fact, trying to look ahead for just two moves in a chess game would generate 1,225 possible chessboard states. Looking ahead 20 moves will generate 2.7 quadrillion possible board states.

To write a computer program to find ways of dealing with the existence of all these possibilities and to be the best in the world at it too is no mean feat. However, there is a severe limit to the intelligence that this style of AI could achieve. Once the knowledge was written into the computer program code, the system could not be updated without going back and changing the code. No matter how many disease cases they diagnosed, or gas pipe fractures they identified, or games of chess they played, GOFAI systems will never improve.

Before we confine GOFAI to the history books, however, it is worth thinking about the uses it still affords. As teachers, we can easily see how a GOFAI system could still be extremely useful in the classroom. For example, planning a school trip involves many possible steps, as illustrated in Figure 1.1. An easy-to-use app that helped

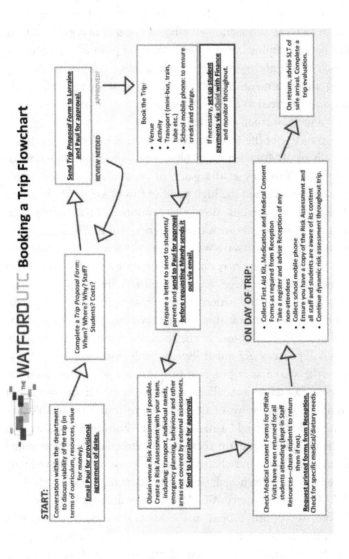

Figure 1.1 An example of the steps involved in planning a trip. (With permission from Paul Quinn, Acting Principal, Watford UTC.)

teachers step through all these processes and decision points could be extremely helpful and it could be built using GOFAI.

It is also worth taking a moment to note that there were suggestions that production rules of the sort used to create systems such as ELIZA and her "offspring" could represent the basis of human thought. For example, the work of John Anderson who developed the adaptive control of thought (ACT) theory of human thought as a set of production rules.[12] As we judge the wisdom of his work, we should remember that we know a great deal more about human thought now than we did at the time that John Anderson was developing his ACT theory. We should also remember that his work precipitated a generation of cognitive STEM tutoring software that was extremely successful at tutoring students in maths and science. Indeed, these cognitive tutoring systems are the basis for the systems that are sold today by the spin-off company from Carnegie Mellon University called Carnegie Learning.[13]

In truth, the Carnegie Learning example was not the zeitgeist in the late 20th and early 21st centuries. From the zenith that was Deep Blue came several decades where AI moved at a much slower pace than it had in the years immediately following the Dartmouth College meeting. The technical limitations of machines that could not learn severely restricted what could be achieved with AI, and funding was less available. The deepest of the AI winters to date was upon us.

MACHINES THAT CAN LEARN

It is always darkest before the dawn so they say, and the AI winter was indeed quite a gloomy time to be working in AI. Progress in AI was slow as we said farewell to the 20th century, and the new millennium dawned. Despite the coolness towards AI, the drive to produce AI systems that, like humans, could become better and better and better at a particular activity was a strong motivator for many aspiring computer scientists. In 2011, Google formed Google Brain and thus emerged the field of machine learning which started to grow.[14]

Machine learning is the approach that many modern AI systems use. Indeed, most of the AI that we use daily is likely, at least in part, to be using machine learning to produce the behaviours that make the system seem intelligent. Imagine, for example, that you have been to a social gathering and seen one of your friends wearing a particular pair of shoes that you really like. Your friend is being coy about where these shoes came from, and how much they cost. But you really want to find out so that you, too, can purchase these shoes whilst at the event. You manage to persuade your friend to let you take a picture of the shoes. This means that you can use that photograph with AI software that is capable of visual search. This type of AI system will search millions and millions and millions of images to try to find an image that matches the shoes in the photograph.

With a bit of luck, the shoes you desire are available on e-commerce sites. If so, it is highly likely that the visual search AI system will be able to find them for you.

Visual search is not just for shoes. It can be a real boon for a teacher too. It is a certainty that, as a teacher, you will be caught out by a question, often a simple one, that you cannot answer. Taking children out to explore, collect, and identify different species of plants, flowers, or trees before sorting and classifying is a common activity. In the vast majority of cases, a child will ask a teacher to name a species of flower, for example, that they may be unfamiliar with. However, help is on hand as there are many apps that utilise visual search AI so that the teacher can take multiple photos, upload them, and get an instant identification. As we said at the start, making friends with AI is a good idea.

TRAINING THE SYSTEM

Systems, such as the visual search systems just described, use machine learning. The instructions within a machine learning AI system, sometimes referred to as the algorithm, need to be trained.[15] In the same way that we as humans can be trained to recognise similarities and differences, AI algorithms can be trained.

The training that enables humans to recognise particular pairs of shoes may not be explicit but it happens as we grow and become more able to see and process the world around us. Every day, as a child grows, they see millions and millions and millions of images from the world around them. The child gradually becomes more accurate at recognising things, mum's face, their own hands, the picture of a whale on the wall next to their cot, for example. In a similar way, the machine learning algorithm must be trained using millions and millions of images of pairs of shoes, or a plant, for example, in order to enable that algorithm to accurately recognise a particular pair of shoes or a plant, when an image is input to the system.

Machine learning AI systems can do many things, not just image recognition visual search. But visual search is one of the activities that machine learning AI is becoming extremely accurate in. Indeed, many of us helped to train these algorithms, mostly, without realizing that we were doing so.

Next time you are signing into a website, and you are asked to select all the instances of a particular item from a set of images (such as staircases, or bridges, or traffic lights),[16] you are helping to label a photograph as containing the item that an algorithm is being trained to recognise. And notice that traffic lights, bridges, staircases, etc. come in a variety of shapes and sizes. Training algorithms to recognise what an image is illustrating is not an easy task. As we will show you in Chapter 5, a great deal of time, and often a great deal of human effort too, is required to prepare the data before a machine learning algorithm can be trained.

PREPARATION IS ESSENTIAL AND HUMAN TIME INTENSIVE

The preparation phase that happens before the machine learning algorithm can start to learn from data requires that data are labelled correctly. Training in order to learn is not just for machines of course. Humans need to do this too. Let's look, for example, at how we learn about shapes. Our world is dominated by shape and space, in the kitchen, in the bathroom, and outside the home. Look around you! It's not hard to see then why geometry is a key part of the component in the programmes of study for maths. Learning about shapes and space enables learners to sort out their visual data in order to think about and describe their environment.

To begin with, children need to have the language, or labels, to name and describe shapes. This normally begins through play. Naming the blocks, spotting and matching the shapes, shape hunts around the school and the local environment are all necessary precursors to understanding future work on measurements, construction perspective in art, and so much more.

This layering of concepts is replicated in machine learning. If the data from which the machine learning algorithm is going to learn are in the form of images and the machine learning needs to be able to identify which of these images contain traffic lights, staircases, shoes, or whatever, then all the images used to train the machine learning algorithm will need to be labelled according to whether or not they contain traffic lights, staircases, or shoes. Who is going to do this labelling? It may be people who work for the company making the AI product, but it may also be you, or me, or our friends as we have just illustrated. The point to note here is that machine learning needs a lot of help from people to even start to learn anything.

LEARNING IS FOR LIFE, EVEN FOR MACHINES

As we have seen, machine learning Artificial Intelligence is built on learning – learning from examples, or more accurately learning from data. The machine learning AI algorithm is given millions and millions of data examples from which it learns. That is, it learns from experience.

The real power of machine learning is found following the training phase. Once the machine learning system has been trained to a level that its developers are confident it is accurate enough to be used in the real world, the system continues to learn and improve.

Again, the same happens with children's learning. Once we have taught them the language of shape and space and they can discriminate and understand the properties of them, they are then ready to go beyond the maths lesson and apply their knowledge to their construction lessons in design and technology. In this way, learners can build upon and consolidate their learning.

TRANSPARENCY AND AI, OR UNDERSTANDING WHAT'S HAPPENING IN THE BLACK BOX

You might be thinking that the advent of machine learning has made GOFAI obsolete, because why use an AI that cannot learn, when you have an AI that can learn? In fact, why even call an AI that cannot learn an AI? There are many people who do not regard GOFAI as AI, and yet it really does come with some significant advantages, despite the rather large disadvantage of not being able to learn. GOFAI creates a trail of decision-making points as its rules are fired. Therefore, any decision that a GOFAI system makes can be explained. This makes GOFAI systems highly transparent.[17]

Machine learning AI, on the other hand, has no rules. It can therefore be extremely hard to know precisely why a machine learning system has made any particular decision. Machine learning AI systems are what we call black box systems.[18] There is no transparency available to show us what the algorithm in the machine learning AI system has done or why it has reached a particular decision. Machine learning is fast, and it learns. It has many advantages over GOFAI. However, the disadvantage of not being able to provide an explanation represents a significant problem, particularly for education and training activities, where it is really important to be able to explain, and often justify, why a particular decision has been made.

In educational settings, it would be a total disaster if you could not explain or justify actions taken. Imagine a situation where peer-on-peer abuse has taken place. The school has investigated and decided upon a course of action that affects one child more than another. In this case, it's your child. On arriving home, the child paints a picture which in your opinion does not justify the action the school has taken. Against this background, and with limited information, every parent would expect and deserve to understand the justification for the decisions made if we expect them to support the actions taken.

GOFAI AND MACHINE LEARNING CAN WORK TOGETHER

The machine learning community is keen to rectify the lack of transparency associated with machine learning AI. Across the world, AI scientists are working on what is often referred to as Explainable AI (XAI).[19] This goal of XAI is to increase the transparency of machine learning AI and find ways to generate explanations and justifications for the decisions these systems make. This may mean blending GOFAI and machine learning techniques to try and get the best of both worlds.

One of the other challenges that machine learning AI faces is the need for enormous amounts of data from which the AI can learn. As an example, let's take an essay grading machine learning AI system. To grade essays accurately that machine learning AI would need to have processed, or "experienced", millions of essays across the full range of possible grades before it can grade essays accurately. Do we have millions of examples of graded essays that cover the full range of possible marks? Are they in a digital format that can be labelled and made accessible to the machine learning AI? We may be able to collate sufficient examples, but it is not easy. The hefty data requirements of machine learning AIs are a key restriction on their application. Not surprisingly, AI scientists are keen to find a way to address this challenge and a new field of machine learning called TinyML[20] is evolving. It is early days for TinyML and it will be interesting to see how successful this new technique may be.

A key component of engaging with AI is to understand the importance of data to machine learning AI. Think about the data you have access to and make a list.

List three kinds of data you have access to.

And

List three tasks you might like an AI to help you with.

As you read this book, think about ways in which an AI might usefully process your data. In the next chapter, we will start to explore the sorts of tasks that AI is better at than we humans are and the tasks that we humans are better at than AI. It would also be useful for you to start thinking about the sorts of tasks that AI might be able to take on to help you.

The data that you think about could be data about individuals, e.g., how they are performing academically. Or perhaps it is data about how those individuals are feeling, whether they are anxious, or whether they are feeling supremely confident. There are many sorts of data available in any organization, and quite often, some of the most obvious kinds of data are not really thought about when we ask the question, what data is available? For example, data about the temperature of a classroom, or about the time it takes people to get from one part of the building to another, or data about light levels in each classroom, or about which pupil regularly sits next to which other pupil.

We appreciate that you are time-poor and thinking about data sources may not seem like a good use of your time. Trust us, it is. In particular, if you are a school leader with many competing demands on your time, it is easy to overlook the value of data. We know that the very fabric of the building and all its resources are important assets in supporting the delivery of learning. To this end, schools have inventories, logbooks, and financial data that document the purchase of everything from PE equipment and technology to the replacement of carpets and even the number of chairs that are ordered. Schools are a treasure trove of underutilised data. Dealing with issues as they arise can be costly and other budgets can suffer as money is pulled from one source to support another. Therefore, schools need to really examine all the data they have, as often the solution to many of the logistical nightmares schools have can be found in the data they hold. And once you know more about your data, you will be much better able to see how AI might help you, through an intelligent repair and maintenance system perhaps. It really is always worth thinking about the sort of data that is and could be available to you in order to make good decisions about where best to deploy AI.

AUTONOMY AND ADAPTIVITY

In this chapter, we have presented a very brief description of the historical roots of today's AI. We have described two main types of AI: GOFAI and machine learning. One type of AI can learn; the other cannot. One type of AI can easily generate explanations for all decisions made, the other cannot. The key concept of data has been delineated, which provides machine learning AI with the experience from which it learns. For the machine learning AI to learn from this data, it must be prepared by people, an activity which many of us participate in unwittingly every day. Finally, in this chapter we want to prepare you for the chapters that follow by introducing you to two characteristics of AI, both machine learning and GOFAI (to an extent), that you will encounter as you read on. These two characteristics are *autonomy* and *adaptivity*[21] and you will see them referred to repeatedly in the rest of this book.

Autonomy is what allows AI systems to complete actions without constant guidance from humans.

Of course, it is important to bear in mind that on some occasions, even if an AI system is capable of behaving autonomously, it may not be desirable for it to do so, for example, autonomous weapons. A balance between autonomy and human guidance is often the best way forward.

Adaptivity describes the way that AI can interact with a person, perhaps to help them learn arithmetic. Adaptivity changes the way that the AI interacts based on the actions the person takes.

In the example of a pupil learning arithmetic, the AI might adapt the difficulty of the arithmetic activities that the pupil is asked to complete, and it might also offer less or more help and support depending upon how easily the pupil is completing the activities. As you read, and the sorts of data that you might have, think about autonomy, and adaptivity too. How could an AI that does not need constant guidance and that can adapt its behaviour be helpful to you?

USEFUL RESOURCES

- Anthony Seldon and Oladimeji Abidoye. The fourth education revolution: will artificial intelligence liberate or infantilise humanity. The University of Buckingham Press.
- Rosemary Luckin. Machine learning and human intelligence: The future of education for the 21st century. UCL Institute of Educational Press.
- Rose Luckin and Wayne Holmes. Intelligence unleashed: An argument for AI in education. Open Ideas at Pearson.
- Barbara Means, Robert Murphy, and Linda Shear. Understand, implement & evaluate. Open Ideas at Pearson.

NOTES

1 https://www.oed.com/viewdictionaryentry/Entry/271625
2 Star Wars' C-3PO.
3 https://en.wikipedia.org/wiki/WALL-E
4 https://en.wikipedia.org/wiki/List_of_Blade_Runner_characters#Roy _Batty
5 https://en.wikipedia.org/wiki/Borg
6 https://en.wikipedia.org/wiki/Ex_Machina_(film)
7 https://academic.oup.com/mind/article/LIX/236/433/986238
   https://scholar.google.com/citations?view_op=list_works&hl=en&hl=en &user=VWCHlwkAAAAJ
8 https://en.wikipedia.org/wiki/Dartmouth_workshop
9 Weizenbaum, J. (1966). ELIZA—a computer program for the study of natural language communication between man and machine. Communications of the ACM, 9(1), 36–45.

10 Of course, we jest, and there were many women who created the conditions for, and pushed the boundaries of, modern computing. See, for example: https://blog.re-work.co/female-data-science-pioneers-you-may-not-have-heard-of/

11 Deep Blue also used another popular GOFAI technique called *Search*. There is insufficient space in this book to give thorough explanation, but as the name suggests Search involves working through possible chessboard states in order to decide which to select. The enormity of the search space for the game of chess means that the team who built the AI had to come up with different techniques to reduce the size of the search space that Deep Blue needed to navigate. You can read about the way Deep Blue worked in this article: https://core.ac.uk/download/pdf/82416379.pdf

12 https://en.wikipedia.org/wiki/ACT-R and Anderson, J. R. (1996). *The Architecture of Cognition* (1st ed.). Psychology Press. https://doi.org/10.4324/9781315799438

13 https://www.actuaries.digital/2018/09/05/history-of-ai-winters/

14 https://www.nytimes.com/2016/12/14/magazine/the-great-ai-awakening.html AND https://en.wikipedia.org/wiki/Google_Brain

15 This description is specific to a very commonly used form of machine learning called supervised machine learning We will discuss this more in Chapter 5, along with some other types of machine learning.

16 https://www.techradar.com/uk/news/captcha-if-you-can-how-youve-been-training-ai-for-years-without-realising-it AND https://towardsdatascience.com/are-you-unwittingly-helping-to-train-googles-ai-models-f318dea53aee AND https://www.google.com/recaptcha/about/

17 https://en.wikipedia.org/wiki/Algorithmic_transparency

18 https://en.wikipedia.org/wiki/Black_box   https://royalsociety.org/-/media/policy/projects/explainable-ai/AI-and-interpretability-policy-briefing.pdf AND https://en.wikipedia.org/wiki/Explainable_artificial_intelligence

19 XAI.

20 https://www.arm.com/blogs/blueprint/tinyml AND https://www.oreilly.com/library/view/tinyml/9781492052036/

21 https://course.elementsofai.com/1/1

2

EDUCATIONAL CHALLENGES AND AI

Curiosity and motivation, as every teacher knows, are key to successful learning. We hope that Chapter 1 helped to "educate, enthuse and excite" you to the history, underpinnings, and possibilities of AI. We now move on to the second step of our AI Readiness Framework, where we explore the challenges educators are facing, and hone our focus to just a few.

WHAT ARE YOUR CHALLENGES?

A key aspect of the AI Readiness approach is to help you focus your thinking on a thorny challenge that you are currently facing as a teacher, headteacher, or possibly a school governor or trustee. Maybe the challenges that you face are systemic and process-based. Or perhaps they are rooted in an attempt to shift your school from a traditional pedagogic approach to an enquiry- or project-based pedagogy.

Before we identify your challenges, let's discuss a recent headline-grabbing challenge, where an attempt to use AI went terribly wrong.

The COVID-19 pandemic cast an existing contemporary challenge for educators, the fairness and accuracy of assessments, particularly examinations-based summative assessments, into even sharper

DOI: 10.1201/9781003193173-2

relief. With pupils unable to attend school, how could (and should) educators assess their progress and award grades? Exam assessments are delivered in a physical space, not online, so when that physical space was unavailable, what then? In England and Wales, an algorithm was used to calculate International Baccalaureate results and national A level and GCSE exam results for 2020. The algorithm made decisions about what exam grade to award in each subject and for each student. The key data that the algorithm used to make grading decisions were the predicted grades made by teachers, and data about the historical performance of the school attended by the student.

The algorithm-produced results caused a massive uproar. The number of A level grade As and above awarded by the algorithm increased by a fairly modest 2.4% compared to 2019.[1] However, 39.1% of A level grades were downgraded from the teacher-assessed grades, with the largest differences being seen for pupils from the lowest socio-economic backgrounds. The algorithm had been designed with a key goal of preventing grade inflation, which it did achieve. However, the influence of the historical data doomed the results of individual students enrolled in historically lower performing schools. The public outrage was such that the grades produced by the algorithm were ignored and the teachers' predicted grades were used instead.

It is important to recognise that this cautionary tale does not mean that algorithms and AI cannot be used for the purpose of decision-support for grades. What it does mean is that the complexity of grading decisions must be recognised and the algorithm must be thoroughly tested before it is allowed to take responsibility for calculating the grades of real students. In addition to which, it should work with teachers, not to revise or replace their grade estimates, but rather to support them when making these estimates with additional data and "number-crunching" power. This would be a good example of AI and Human Intelligence (HI) working together.

When identifying your own challenges, cast your net wide. Think about challenges of all different sorts. For example, challenges that are never far from any educator's mind are those concerned with insuring student well-being and mental health, another growing area of concern. Climate change and the environment, and preparing students to address these urgent needs, is high on the list of many educators' challenges. Social mobility is a continuing area of attention, as are worries about those involved in university admissions who must ensure that they do not discriminate against categories of students as they design and apply their admissions policies. Questions designed to address additional challenges school teachers and headteachers might be facing are listed in Exhibits X and Y, as well as an empty list (Exhibit Z) for you to start to jot down some of your own questions and challenges. Might some of these problems be addressed through the judicious development and application of AI?[2]

EXHIBIT X: QUESTIONS TO HELP IDENTIFY CHALLENGES THAT A SCHOOL TEACHER MIGHT BE FACING

- Are the children in my class attending regularly?
- Have the children developed good relationships amongst their peers?
- Are the children in my class well nourished?
- Have I planned lessons that meet the expected learning outcomes?
- Does my marking and feedback effectively engage students such that they act to improve their learning?
- How do I evaluate parental perceptions of me as a teacher?
- How do I ensure that soft skills are developed by my students?
- How do I know that we are meeting the expected standards for teaching and learning?
- What should I do to close the gender gap in maths?

EXHIBIT Y: QUESTIONS TO HELP IDENTIFY CHALLENGES THAT HEADTEACHERS MIGHT BE FACING

- How do I recruit and retain the right staff for my context?
- How do I source or develop CPD to meet the needs of my staff?
- How do I build ed tech capacity amongst my staff?
- How do I ensure my students with special education needs receive the provision they need?
- How do I ensure we meet our aspirational targets for core academic subjects?
- How do I know that I'm communicating in a timely manner with all stakeholders?
- How can I assess if my school development plan is fit for purpose?
- How can I see if all children across the school are making progress?
- How will I know that the school is getting a good return on the investments we are making?[3]

TEN QUESTIONS TO HELP YOU DECIDE WHICH CHALLENGE (OR CHALLENGES) TO FOCUS ON

Clearly, there are a plethora of possible challenges. Now that you've started to articulate some of your own, it's time to start to focus. To help you decide which of your set of challenges is the best one to focus on first, we have developed a set of ten questions.

Ask these of yourself, your colleagues, team, peers, managers or stakeholders, and use the answers to narrow your pool.

1   What do you already know about this challenge? [Score 3 if you know a great deal, Score 2 if a modest amount, Score 1 if you don't know much, and Score 0 if you know nothing about this at all]

2 What kind of information is it possible for you to know that you don't know now? For example, if you are wanting to know more about the attainment gaps between different pupil groups, think hard about exactly what you could know about the pupils, their friends, family, context, etc. Or, perhaps you are concerned about bullying – there are different types of bullying in different degrees. For example, cyber, physical, name-calling, etc. It would be possible for you to explore the environmental conditions in the school that allow for these incidents to happen. [*Score 3 if you are confident that you could know a great deal more, Score 2 if you believe that you could know a modest amount more, Score 1 if you are not sure that there is a great deal more that you could know, and Score 0 if you believe there is nothing more that you could know*]

3 To what extent is the challenge you are facing controllable, and by whom? Are all systems and procedures understood clearly by all staff teaching and support? Are they audited, reported, and monitored? [*Score 3 if the challenge is (a) controllable, (b) by someone at the school or within the school group, and (c) you do have all the systems in place to control the challenge; Score 2 if any two of (a), (b), and (c) are true; Score 1 if any one of (a), (b), and (c) is true; and Score 0 if none of (a), (b), or (c) is true*]

For example, recruiting, training, and maintaining the best staff team. Any organisation only has limited control over the recruitment challenge, because whilst it can optimise all elements of the recruitment process that it adopts it cannot control how many people apply. Hopefully you have confidence that there are systems in place to help you optimise the elements of the recruitment process that are within your control, and AI can certainly help with that. However, the organisation cannot alter the number of people who are looking for the sort of employment that is on offer. Similarly, the school cannot control the pool of applicants that have the appropriate qualifications, skills, and expertise for the roles that need to be filled. [*In this example, the score would be 2, because the whole of the recruitment process*] is not under your control, but you do have the systems in place to maximise the aspects of the process that are within your control]

4   What level of uncertainty is there? There may well be a level of uncertainty with a challenge based on incomplete reporting procedures by staff and children, for example, or due to a challenge being surfaced through anecdotal evidence. [Score 3 if the level of uncertainty is negligible, Score 2 if there is a modest amount of uncertainty, Score 1 if there is a great deal of uncertainty, and Score 0 if there is no certainty at all]

5   Do you already have any data to help you understand this challenge or can you access data about this? [Score 3 if you have or can access a large amount of data from different sources, Score 2 if you have or can access a modest amount of data from different sources, Score 1 if you have or can access a very little data from any source, and Score 0 if you neither have, not have access to any data]For example, you might have data derived from existing surveys, parent comments or complaints, behaviour logs and risk assessments.

6   Can you collect more data if you don't have enough data to help you understand this challenge and work out how best to tackle it? There are always opportunities to collect more data from students. [Score 3 if you can collect a large amount of relevant data, Score 2 if you can collect a modest amount of relevant data, Score 1 if you can only collect a small amount of relevant data, and Score 0 if you are unable to collect any new data at all]

7   How accurate can you be in your assessment of the challenge and your prediction about the best way to tackle it? [Score 3 if you can be very accurate, Score 2 if you can be quite accurate, and Score 1 if you can only be imprecise and therefore not very accurate at all, and Score 0 if you cannot be accurate at all]

    For example, cyber bullying is a challenge that can be difficult to assess accurately, because it can occur outside of school grounds and systems.

8   Do you or your organisation have the appetite and capability to change to address this challenge? [Score 6 if the answer is "yes" and Score 0 if the answer is "no"]

If the answer is no, for whatever reason, it may not be a good investment of your time to be looking at ways AI can help you tackle the challenges in new ways.

9   Is the challenge AI compatible? [*Score 3 if it is very AI compatible, Score 2 if it is modestly compatible, Score 1 if it is not very compatible, and Score 0 if it is completely incompatible*]

This may be a difficult question for you to answer at the moment, but the section of this chapter entitled "Who has got the power, Artificial or Human Intelligence?" will help, as we hope will the rest of the book.

10   Finally, and most importantly, how important is solving this challenge to you or to your organisation? [*Score 6 if it is crucial to solve this challenge, Score 4 if it is important to solve this challenge, Score 2 if it is quite important, and Score 0 if it is not important at all*]

The challenge that scores the highest should be your priority. If you have more than one challenge with the highest score then prioritise questions 8 and 10, by doubling their scores.

Whatever your key challenges, be they recruitment, retention of staff, training, or something completely different, you may need to select between the challenges that remain after you have probed them with the ten questions. The ten questions are there to prompt you to think about your particular situation with respect to each of the questions and the activity should be seen as a guiding tool and not a doctrine.

One of our aims in writing this book, and of AI Readiness more generally, is to ensure that educators understand enough about AI to make wise decisions when deciding how much of their financial resources should be allocated to AI technology. However, in making these decisions, it is important to *recognise that AI alone will rarely yield a solution. Far more likely, it will be AI and HI working hand-in-hand to achieve a solution.*

UNDERSTANDING YOUR ASSUMPTIONS

A further process that is extremely useful when you have worked through the ten questions activity is to make explicit the assumptions that underlie the answer you gave to each question. It is important to specify your assumptions even if you have managed to prioritise one challenge. If you have more than one challenge that has the same score after the ten questions activity, then making your assumptions explicit can help you differentiate which challenge to prioritise first.

It can be hard to make your assumptions explicit – they are after all assumptions, often unwritten best guesses that we have never formalised.

For example, perhaps you have set yourself a challenge to ensure that every student has access to a computer at home, because you are rolling out an AI platform that provides individualised lessons that adapt to each pupil's needs and that is compatible with your curriculum. You want to be well prepared if there are future disruptions such as those that happened during the COVID-19 pandemic. You find local businesses who are willing to help with sponsorship of the technology, and your deputy head's wife is a computer whizz who has offered to help too. But, have you checked your assumptions? Are you assuming that all parents will want their child to have a computer at home, that there is a quiet space for the child to work at home and that the home has broadband connectivity adequate enough for the proposed AI platform? Are you assuming what the local businesses who are sponsoring the technology will want in return, advertising perhaps? Are those businesses involved in activities that all parents would feel appropriate for a school sponsorship arrangement?

We all make assumptions all the time, so get yours out in the open and clearly described and recorded.

WHO HAS THE POWER: ARTIFICIAL OR HUMAN INTELLIGENCE?

With question nine, we asked you to delve into AI compatibility and promised to explain more in this chapter section. We are keeping our promise now. In order to understand whether AI would be useful in helping with a particular challenge, we need to know the activities that are best done by an AI, and those that are best done by humans. Table 2.1 illustrates some of the areas at which AI reigns supreme and some of the activities at which Human Intelligence (HI) is still very much the master.[4]

The differences between AI and HI give each type of intelligence the opportunity to excel over the other. For example, AI's power makes it capable of delivering one-to-one tutoring systems that generate activities targeted at individual learner's needs and provide timely feedback on micro-steps of learning so that students can work at their own pace. These intelligent tutoring systems can process enormous amounts of data in a way that would take teachers hours, days, weeks to synthesise to make appropriate decisions about learning content. AI does not tire, nor does it need to sleep or eat, so AI can provide learning that is always on, personalised and inclusive and free up teachers to design the lesson approach.

However, one of AI's weaknesses is social intelligence. Unlike the human teacher, AI cannot make empathetic adjustments for students who may have started the day in an emotional state and find it hard to engage even with concepts with which they are familiar, or a learner who you know needs the social interaction of a teacher for support.

BRINGING ETHICS INTO THE ASSESSMENT

Before we move on further, it is important to take a moment to consider the ethical implications of any data-driven process that involves AI. This is not always easy given the complexity of AI. However, AI's complexity can be simplified by breaking down the questions that need to be considered in the following areas.

ETHICS AND DATA

Was the decision to collect data made ethically? Has the data been collected with the full consent of the people whose data it is? Is the data being stored securely? Is it private and protected and are we

Table 2.1   Some of the Strengths of Artificial and Human Intelligence

What can AI do better than us?	What can we do better than AI?
Pattern matching	Interdisciplinary academic intelligence
Classification of objects into particular groupings	Meta-knowing intelligence: the ability to recognise and generate good evidence on which decisions can be made about whether or not information is true
Automating and replicating repetitive tasks	
Processing large amounts of data	
Storing large amounts of data	Social intelligence
Collecting and integrating data from multiple locations and sensors, some of which may be monitoring biological systems	Meta-cognitive intelligence: the ability to plan, monitor, and regulate our own thinking
Reduce complex phenomena to pieces that can be understood by people	Meta-subjective intelligence: the ability to recognise and monitor our development of emotional intelligence and that of others with whom we interact
	Meta-contextual intelligence: the ability to move seamlessly between different locations, people, places, and environments
	Perceived self-efficacy[5]

making sure that other people can't access this data unless they are someone to whom there is express permission for access?

ETHICS AND PROCESSING

Will that processing of the data be done in a way that will reduce the possibility of bias in the way in which the date is processed? Do we feel confident that the processing of the data will produce fair and appropriate outputs?

ETHICS AND OUTPUTS

What is the output from the AI's processing of data? The output might be considered to be the final piece of the ethical puzzle for any AI application. However, sometimes an output is also an input for the next phase of processing, and therefore it is not the final piece of the puzzle.

Let us look at an example of the questioning that might take place as a process of ethical AI thinking progresses.

In the UK, children with special educational needs (SENs) may have either an education, health, and care plan (EHCP) or an individual education plan (IEP) that sets out the goals they have for the year and any support they will need to achieve them. To monitor each child's progress teachers must make decisions about the data that is relevant to each goal. Analysis of this data at regular intervals leads to instructional decision-making for the next sequence of learning. This iterative cycle continues as the student makes progress and allows for corrections in approach in response to social, emotional, and environmental changes, such as transitioning between school years or schools. In each case, a further cycle of questioning about data collection and processing begins.[6] If we wanted to introduce AI into such a process, we would need to take the same steps as we do for the manual process. We must be sure the decision to collect data has been made ethically, that it has been collected with full consent, that it is stored securely and protected so that only those authorised can access this data. We will discuss more about ethics in Chapter 7.

GETTING TO KNOW YOUR DATA

As we come to the end of this chapter, take a moment to reflect on some of the questions that it has raised about data.

- What are all the various ways that you and your colleagues come into contact with data (e.g., do you use smart sensing systems to monitor the use of electricity through heat and light, for instance)? What data might be available from these systems?
- What data and process steps do you go through in your day-to-day activities (e.g., when arranging a trip that involves travel and accommodation for the students)? Could AI help you with this?

We can always learn more about the challenges we face from our data. For example, you can compare a school's overall results to national standards, highlighting areas of strength and those that need further investigation. This data can be filtered further to look at the performance of specific groups of students, such as students from different socio-economic backgrounds. We can perhaps keep an eye towards analysing whether the additional funds spent on training the teaching and support staff have resulted in improved progress for the students. All of this can be done without AI but imagine how much more quickly and effectively it might be done if we had AI to help us complete some of these tasks.

School staff who work in human resources or in finance also come into contact with a great deal of data that is extremely important when it comes to learning about the challenges that schools face. It is therefore extremely important that not just teaching staff, but all staff in a school understand why data is so important to machine learning AI. As discussed in Chapter 1, data is the experience through which a machine learning algorithm learns and makes decisions about what actions to take.

GETTING READY FOR CHAPTER 3

As a final thought, as we move on to Chapter 3, consider the sorts of data that you come into contact with frequently and those that you rarely encounter. The questions in Figure 2.1 might help prompt your thinking. Perhaps, also start to think about the sort of data that you could be collecting that might be useful, but that you are not collecting at the moment. Could you be more effective at connecting the different data that you already have or that you could access in the future to help you understand a great deal more about your challenges? For example, schools are under tremendous pressure to collect data that shows student progress over time. In the main, this evidence is achieved through the analysis of ongoing assessments from daily work, quizzes and tests, and eventually terminal exams. However, we know from research[7] that deeper learning occurs when the activities planned are more collaborative and are more active, social, and contextual, with greater student ownership and engagement. And yet, schools rarely collect data which focuses on the collaborative, active, and contextualised nature of learning or even a small aspect of it, such as the balance of teacher talk to student talk. There are any number of useful, small first steps to collect extra data, just like this example of teacher and student talk, that could be taken.

If you work in education or training

What data do you have about the sessions you have planned and how well they have been received?

What kind of technology do you use?

Do you look at learning analytics feedback?

How do you connect data about planning and execution of teaching with assessment data?

Could you be learning more from your data?

Figure 2.1   Questions to ask yourself about data.

We hope that you have found Chapter 2 thought provoking and that you have identified some of the challenges that you face as a teacher or headteacher. Chapter 3 will continue to progress through the AI Readiness Framework and will consider further the relationship between an identified challenge and the data that need to be collated or collected in order to better understand that challenge from the data perspective.

USEFUL RESOURCES

Solved! Making the case for collaborative problem-solving. Rose Luckin, Ed Baines, Mutlu Cukurova, and Wayne Holmes, with Michael Mann: https://media.nesta.org.uk/documents/solved-making-case-collaborative-problem-solving.pdf

Three questions with Turing Lecturer Rose Luckin:

https://www.turing.ac.uk/blog/three-questions-turing-lecturer-rose-luckin

NOTES

1 Passing grades for A level are, from highest to lowest, A*, A, B, C, D, and E. Those who do not reach the minimum standard required for a grade E receive the non-grade U (unclassified).

2 Some of the challenges you face will be more appropriate for AI than others. As you progress through this book, you will be better able to decide which sorts of challenge might be best addressed using AI techniques and tools.

3 When thinking about challenges, it is always important to think about value for money. The amount of money that is available to be spent on any kind of technology, including AI, is not great in most schools, which makes it even more important that money is spent on the right AI resources.

4 It is important to bear in mind that any challenge you select will likely involve multiple tasks, each with multiple steps. The point at which it becomes clear where AI would be more helpful than HI, or vice versa, may be buried deep within the sub-steps of these multiple tasks. So, don't worry if you are not yet able to decide about what sort of intelligence might be best suited to any aspect of your challenge.

5 Perceived self-efficacy is one of the key elements of our own Human Intelligence and it is explained in this book. https://www.ucl-ioe-press.com /books/education-and-technology/machine-learning-and-human-intelligence/There are several videos that explain the concept as well, for example: https://www.youtube.com/watch?v=P33FRjJWh4E

6 As in some of the previous examples we present, the current process we describe does not involve AI, but it very well could benefit from AI and the same ethical questions would need to be asked, and more as we shall see in Chapter 7, when we talk more about ethics and AI in education.

7 https://media.nesta.org.uk/documents/solved-making-case-collaborative -problem-solving.pdf

3

DATA, DATA EVERYWHERE

The focus of this chapter is data – what it is and how its value can be identified. In education and training, there are many sources of data that are well known and used. There are also many sources of data that are less well known, as well as many types of data that are not collected at all, but that could be very useful, particularly for AI to process. There is an understandable reticence about data collection within education: a worry that people who should not be able to access the data collected will see it, or that it will be misused. It is therefore extremely important that ethics is at the forefront of our thinking when data collection and collation are being considered.

After reading this chapter, you should be able to identify the sources of data that are relevant to your work and life, particularly those that are important for the challenge that you identified in Chapter 2. You will also understand the differences between a range of data sources. Multimodal data will be introduced and explained, and its value will be discussed, as will the advantages and disadvantages that it entails. The challenges that can accompany its collection, use, and application are also described. This chapter should help you to identify the data that are relevant to your challenge(s). We'll show you the importance of knowing where data is stored, how it is stored, how it is structured, who is responsible for the data, how it can be accessed, and why it is important to your challenge.

DOI: 10.1201/9781003193173-3

WHY SO MUCH TALK ABOUT DATA?

As we have shown you in Chapter 2, modern AI that uses a machine learning approach requires data in order to learn. We want you to understand what AI is and how it works, without "getting into the weeds" of the technical details. Therefore, we are taking you through a step-by-step process, chapter by chapter, to show you how AI could process the sort of data that you have access to. In this way, we hope to show you what you could learn from an AI about the sort of educational challenge that you could be facing. At the same time, we hope that you will understand more about AI, so that you are better able to select the most appropriate AI to purchase in the future. You might like to think about our approach in this book as encouraging you to "get inside" a machine learning algorithm as it were to be part of the same steps that are broadly adopted when a machine learning system is designed, created, and applied, in order to understand what machine learning is all about.

Pretty neat, don't you think?

WHAT EXACTLY IS DATA?

Data is everywhere. From the information that we read in newspapers and magazines, whether they are in paper form or online, to the staff records that every employer keeps about their workforce, the meter readings that we submit to our electricity or gas supplier so they can calculate the money we should be charged, and the scores that our students achieve in assessments as they learn various parts of the curriculum. These are all data.

DATA IN EDUCATION

Data in education might be about the physical learning environment, the virtual learning environment, the curriculum, the pedagogy, the use of resources, and much more besides. In addition, the connections that exist between these factors are also a form of data, as is, the connections that exist between these factors and the people who are learning. Much of this data is invisible to the majority of people. For example, the connection between the staff and students at your school and the computer in the library can be used to search for the shelf location of a book. How many of them use this computer, when, for how long? Or, perhaps you have bought a range of software packages over the past few years. How many staff and students use each of these software packages? How long for? When? Could any of these software packages help you to collect data about how they are being used, whether or not they are effective, etc.? Being able to recognise and identify data sources, both potential and actual, is an important part of becoming AI Ready.

BACK TO MACHINE LEARNING AI

We now know that machine learning AI relies on data. In addition to the existence of machine learning AI, there is another reason that data has become such an important topic over the past decade. Quite simply, there are now so many new ways of collecting data. For example, data is collected from fitness devices that many people wear on their wrists; it is collected by the facial and voice recognition systems that are used to identify people and save them needing to remember a password; and data is constantly collected through the increasing levels of surveillance across big cities, including through video doorbells that can scan the street in front of them as well as the person at the door.

Data is processed in lots of different ways. We look for trends and patterns. We investigate data to find out answers to questions, such as did all our students achieve the grades that we expected them to achieve? Data is used to inform the decisions that we make as a teacher. For example, if I want to find some additional resources to teach students about seed distribution, I might look at several of the many online resource repositories and peruse the reviews that my peers have awarded available resources. I can then use this data to inform the decision I make about the resources I will use with my students.

CONNECTING CHALLENGES
TO DATA SOURCES

In Chapter 2, we discussed the importance of identifying a challenge as the focus of attention as we work through the process of becoming AI Ready. One challenge many of you are likely considering is the question of how you can know that you are maintaining the quality of teaching and learning when some students are learning face to face in school, some students are learning at home using technology, and the situation is constantly changing over time. We could therefore ask the question: what can data tell us that can help us to know if and how we ensure the quality of teaching and learning in a class, in a year group, in a school?

Every challenge can be unpacked into two questions that can help when trying to identify the data we need:

1. What data does previous research give about this challenge – can I learn from this research about the sort of data that I should collect?
2. What data do I have access to that will be relevant to this challenge?

Teachers, trainers, and academic researchers are all interested in understanding and improving the teaching and learning processes that they use. They are usually also interested in improving the outcomes of the students who they teach.

There are therefore many, many research papers that indicate that teaching and learning outcomes are the result of interactions between a range of factors, including, for example:

- The learner's prior knowledge
- The learner's emotions
- The learner's motivation
- Contextual factors in which the learners and educators interact[1]

AN EXAMPLE OF THE SORT OF DATA
THAT IS RELEVANT TO A CHALLENGE

Let's be more specific and work through an example. One of the ways that teaching might be happening, either online or face to face, is through collaborative problem-solving (CPS). There is already a significant amount of research literature about CPS for us to draw on.[2] Now we want to identify potential data sources to help us use machine learning to understand if a group of students are effectively collaborating or if they need some help from their teacher.

Some useful sources of research findings include the following:

Synchrony: students' visual synchrony, measured with eye trackers, is positively correlated with students' learning.[3]

Individual accountability: group goals and individual accountability are two key features found in successful groups.[4]

Equality: two-way dialogue, taking direction from one another, is positively correlated with effective CPS.[5]

Intra-individual variability: can indicate the creation of a common ground among group members based on students' ability to understand.[6]

What can we learn from this research that will help us to identify potential data sources? The first research finding that relates to the synchrony of each student's eye gaze direction, suggests that eye tracking technology could be a useful tool for collecting data. These devices were once extremely expensive, but they are now relatively affordable. The data from the eye tracking technology can be automatically captured in a non-invasive manner and then passed to a machine learning algorithm that processes the data to identify when and how often a group of students are looking at each other or are looking at the same thing – hopefully the problem they are trying to solve! In other words, the students' eye gaze displays synchrony. This may not be a type of data people would have considered previously; however, it can be extremely useful.

WHERE TO LOOK FOR DATA

The previous example demonstrates that research findings can point us in the right direction when it comes to identifying the sort of data that will help us to better understand the educational challenge that is the focus of our attention as we work through the AI Readiness process. The eye tracking example also illustrates that data sources may not be immediately obvious, and it is therefore useful to think as broadly as possible when you are looking for data sources. For example, perhaps you have access to some of these data sources:

- Data showing the balance between teacher talk and student talk
- Temperature check records to measure the optimal environmental conditions for students and teachers
- Peer reviews
- Benchmarking data to examine processes and models at other schools to adapt techniques and approaches
- Staff recruitment and retention, including data about the surrounding area routes to key cities, cost of housing locally, etc.
- Questionnaires – parents, students, and staff
- Externally generated reports for awards, such as Ofsted, LEA in the UK
- Behaviour logs
- Use and types of manipulatives, compared to students' abilities and needs
- Attendance
- Data about movements, such as student keyboard or mouse movements, or throwing arms and jumping in PE lessons to allow for evaluation and development
- Performance reviews
- Social media/newspaper reviews
- Governor/trust reflection, feedback, and reports
- Emergency drills and simulations

There are so many different kinds of data that could be collected. It may seem like an enormous challenge to work out where best to focus when answering the question: what data sources should we collect and use?

A useful approach when exploring potential data is to ask yourself what data you already have in hand:

- Who are the people in your organisation, including members of staff at all different levels, sub-contractors, and administrative staff?
- What is the physical or virtual environment, the offices, the training site, laboratories, exercise spaces, catering spaces, living spaces?
- What are the resources, such as books, technology, equipment, and financial resources, that are being used?

Once you have asked yourself these questions and identified some of the data sources that are available, then it is important to look to see if there are any connections between these different data sources, and if there is also data about these connections.

Returning to the example of maintaining the quality of teaching and learning processes, data that will help us to understand students' baseline knowledge or their emotions and motivation could be useful and available or easy to collect. In addition, there could be information about the nature of the environment where teaching and learning interactions take place. Is it too hot, noisy, or cold? Does the lighting in the classroom accommodate the students' visual needs or does it hinder them?[7]

One of the recurring issues that draws the attention of school leaders and staff at all levels is the gender gap between boys and girls in particular subject areas such as maths, for example. In these cases, several questions spring to mind, as do a host of potential data sources.

WHAT DO YOU NEED TO UNDERSTAND?

GENERAL

- Is the gender gap for maths always present, or does it emerge in certain situations, like summative assessments?
- How good is the subject Leadership of this subject across different teams, departments, and the whole school?

STAFF

- Do the teachers' perceptions of their learners affect the outcomes?
- What is the balance of teacher-student talk for male and female students, and what is the effect? Are both groups given enough time to reflect, shape, and respond to questions asked?
- Does the hidden curriculum affect the different genders' learning behaviour in this area, i.e., social cues, facial expression, body language, voice pitch and tone, and personal space and boundaries?

STUDENTS

- What is the student's readiness to learn – mindset/confidence levels – compared to outcomes?

PARENTS

- Do parental perceptions of a subject affect the child's approach – "I'm not good at maths, and she/he takes after me"?

ENVIRONMENT

- Does the environment in which the students learn maths have a positive/negative effect – e.g., setting/not setting, numbers of learners in a class, or the ratio of boys to girls?

RESOURCES

- Are the resources appropriate and differentiated to meet the needs of the students?

DATA SOURCES

- Assessments and test data for children across the school, year group, and classes
- The balance of SEND between genders
- Performance review of subject leader and class teachers regarding subject expertise
- Pupil conferences
- Data analysis comparing setting groups with non-setting groups
- School report together with reflections from parents' comments
- Parental meeting notes
- Observations and monitoring review notes of teaching and learning
- Analysis of teacher–student talk
- Video-enabled professional learning platform
- Comparison of attendance data
- Action research reports

MULTIMODAL DATA

WHAT IS MULTIMODAL DATA?

The examples of the data discussed so far include examples that are collected from different modalities of human communication: eye tracking, audio recording, gesture recognition and tracking, and logging mouse movements. This variety of data sources that considers all the human senses is called multimodal data. Modes are channels of information, e.g., audio, visual, speech, or movement, and they have become increasingly valuable data points when applying AI.

Let's take a moment to explore more about multimodal data: what it is, how can it be used, and what are its relative advantages and disadvantages.

HOW DOES MULTIMODAL DATA RELATE TO AN EDUCATIONAL CHALLENGE?

For any challenge, all the data that can be brought together under the term "multimodal" must be semantically connected in some way. For example, one sort of data might be complementary to another sort of data. That is, using multiple modes of data can help identify patterns that were not visible when working with data from only one modality: speech data provides valuable additional information about a person's changing emotions that facial expression data alone cannot. One source of data complements the other. It is important to recognise, however, that the behaviours that we can observe are just a part of the picture when it comes to trying to understand something as complex as learning behaviour.

For example, a student may not be looking at the work that they are supposed to be completing. They are instead looking distracted, as if to daydream. This is a useful piece of information, but without additional different information, such as the fact that this student has a habit of looking away from their work when they are working out what to do next, we cannot deduce a great deal about the student's behaviour.

THE OBSERVABLE AND THE HYPOTHESIS DATA SPACE

We can think about all this data that can be collected about the observable aspects of human behaviour as the input space for the analysis that needs to be done to understand higher-order processes, such as cognition, motivation, beliefs, and emotions.

There is also a second space that can be referred to as the hypothesis space. This is the space that connects data sources to features of learning using what might be called learning labels. For example, to assure the quality of teaching and learning in an institution, perhaps in particular the teaching and learning activities that relate to collaborative problem-solving, we might collect data about where our students are looking and how their hands are moving as they work together to build a bird table that can withstand the determined behaviour of the local squirrels. We have data about students' eye gaze direction, and we have data about the movements of their hands. This data is the observable evidence that we have to work with. It is part of the input space.

But how is data about eye gaze and hand movements connected to the complex process of collaborative problem-solving? How can the input space tell us something useful about collaborative problem-solving?

As described earlier, previous research into collaborative problem-solving has indicated that students looking at each other or at the same thing, such as the object of their activity, is a possible signifier for effective collaborative problem-solving. This relationship between the synchrony of students' eye gaze and collaborative problem-solving can be described as a correlation. There is also a correlation between the synchrony of students' hand movements and their ability to perform collaborative problem-solving effectively. The observable data can be connected to the learning labels that we wish to identify. In this example, collaborative problem-solving, is used to build a hypothesis space that connects the observable evidence with the learning that we wish to observe.

CONNECTING THE DOTS THROUGH MULTIPLE DATA SOURCES

Now, it is of course true that merely identifying hand movements and eye gaze is not in and of itself sufficient evidence to draw the conclusion that a particular group of students are, or not, collaborating effectively. However, there is good evidence to support a hypothesis that this observable data could be an excellent indicator of student collaboration that could contribute to a collection of indicators. Together these indicators would be able to tell us something more conclusive about the collaborative problem-solving of a group of students.

A further example of the usefulness of multimodal data for analysing and learning about student learning can be seen in the Java Tutor at North Carolina State University.[8]

The project that developed the Java Tutor produced an extremely large data set that included data from log files recorded as students were using computers to work together to solve problems. There was also facial expressions data, data about student posture and gesture, and even skin conductivity traces. All this data was collated and analysed to learn about measures of effectiveness, learning gains, and student emotion, motivation, and engagement. The research team at North Carolina State found that students' beliefs in their own abilities could have implications for the types of adaptive support that is most suited to their needs. For example, giving students more control is likely to be more effective for high self-efficacy students, along with social dialogue too, whereas, low self-efficacy students are more likely to flourish if they are provided with a guided experimentation approach.[9]

ADVANTAGES AND DISADVANTAGES OF MULTIMODAL DATA SOURCES

The examples discussed in this chapter illustrate some of the advantages that multimodal data brings. Firstly, it can be of great benefit when attempting to recognise the social reality of educational organisations, which involve complex processes with a combination of skills, abilities, and knowledge. In other words, they are multidimensional. Secondly, multimodal data can be used to recognise that the constructs involved in teaching and learning are not necessarily static processes: they change over time. In other words, they are temporal. Thirdly, student learning happens in situ[10] and is not necessarily constrained to a specific physical or digital space. Students could be learning at home, at school, and in places in between. Further, learning is contextualised. Therefore, a single data source that solely focuses on the interactions that occur between learners and a specific teacher, for example, without also considering the environment and the other people who are part of it will not be sufficient to reflect the complexity of the learning context. Multiple multimodal data sources can help provide valuable information about a learning context.

BALANCING MULTIPLE DATA FACTORS

As this chapter draws to a close, it is important to recognise that collating the different data sources that you have identified is a balancing act. We need to balance factors, such as data quality and quantity, against the extent to which the data sources available really do address our focused challenge.

It may be that to capture the most accurate and tightly focused data, we would need to be very intrusive. For example, say the challenge we had decided to focus upon was to explore the impact of neurodiversity among students in a class where there are behaviour challenges. Then the most accurate and focused data source might be achieved by having all the students wear special caps that monitor their neural functioning. Over a period of days, students who have particular diverse needs, such as dyslexia, dyscalculia, or ADHD, may be identified. This could be extremely useful. However, the process of gathering this data would be extremely intrusive for the students involved.

We would therefore also need to consider other, less intrusive data sources that could also help us understand why this particular class has more behavioural challenges than others. Data sources that do not need to be collected in such an intrusive manner might, for example, include multimodal data that can help provide valuable information about each student's context, and ensure that we are not relying on one single data source too heavily. Relying on a single data source is risky because it may turn out to be less reliable than originally thought. Perhaps, for example, the calibration of the special caps that collected the data about students' neural behaviour was faulty. So, not only would the use of these caps have been intrusive, but it would also have been ineffective.

Finally, it is important to ensure that we avert the danger of the "street light effect" when selecting data sources. This effect is grounded in the image of a drunk person who has lost their car keys and is looking for them under the light of a streetlamp. They are behaving in this way because it is easier for them to see in this area than that which is poorly lit, even though the last time the keys were in their possession they were in the poorly lit area.

MOVING ON FROM FINDING EXISTING DATA TO COLLECTING NEW DATA

It is not always the best idea to select data sources that are easiest to access. Many times, it is worth going to a little more trouble to access data sources that are of the greatest relevance to our challenge. We hope that this chapter has explained the different types of data that may be available to you and that could help you to understand more about the challenge you have identified. You have now tackled Step 3 in the AI Readiness programme, well done. Please keep the data sources that you have started to think about in mind as you move on to Chapter 4, in which we will discuss how you could collect some more data to complement the data you have already identified and accessed.

NOTES

1 See, for example, Dumas, D. G., McNeish, D., & Greene, J. A. (2020). Dynamic measurement: A theoretical-psychometric paradigm for modern educational psychology. *Educational Psychologist.* Available here: https://www.researchgate.net/profile/Denis-Dumas-3/publication/339849196_Dynamic_Measurement_A_Theoretical-Psychometric_Paradigm_for_Modern_Educational_Psychology/links/5e69117592851c2408926532/Dynamic-Measurement-A-Theoretical-Psychometric-Paradigm-for-Modern-Educational-Psychology.pdf

2 There is a significant amount of literature about collaborative problem solving (CPS). This report contains many relevant and useful links to this

work: https://media.nesta.org.uk/documents/solved-making-case-col-laborative-problem-solving.pdf

3 Schneider, B., & Pea, R. (2013). Real-time mutual gaze perception enhances collaborative learning and collaboration quality. *International Journal of Computer-Supported Collaborative Learning*, 8, 375–397.

4 Slavin, R. E. (1991). Synthesis of research of cooperative learning. *Educational Leadership*, 48, 71–82.

5 Damon, W., & Phelps, E. (1989). Critical distinctions among three approaches to peer education. *International Journal of Educational Research*, 13, 9–19. AND Dillenbourg, P., Lemaignan, S., Sangin, M., Nova, N., & Molinari, G. (2016). The symmetry of partner modelling. *International Journal of Computer-Supported Collaborative Learning*, 11, 227–253.

6 Marlowe, H. A. (1986). Social intelligence: Evidence for multidimensionality and construct independence. *Journal of Educational Psychology*, 78, 52.

7 http://www.heppell.net/lighting/

8 http://projects.intellimedia.ncsu.edu/javatutor/multimodal-data-analytics/

9 Wiggins, J., Grafsgaard, J., Boyer, K. E., Wiebe, E., & Lester, J. (2017). Do you think you can? The influence of student self-efficacy on the effectiveness of tutorial dialogue for computer science. *International Journal of Artificial Intelligence in Education*, 27(1), 130–153.

10 Sharples, M., & Roschelle, J. (2010). Guest editorial, special section on mobile and ubiquitous technologies for learning. *IEEE Transactions on Learning Technologies*, 3(1), 4–6.

4

LOOKING AT DATA DIFFERENTLY

In Chapter 3, we discussed the sort of data sources that might be available within a school or college, and how to identify them. We also explained the nature of multimodal data and its advantages and disadvantages, as well as the need for balance when selecting data. The purpose for discussing data and using machine learning on that data, as we shall do in Chapter 5, is to understand the challenge you have selected (Chapter 2) and in so doing, you will understand a great deal more about how AI works, what it can do, and what it can't do. Using AI to understand a particular challenge is the first step towards understanding how best AI can be leveraged to address the challenge.

Following on from the discussion about the different types of data that may already be available within an education setting in Chapter 3, the focus of this chapter is on identifying and collecting new data. The data in question is data that is relevant to the challenge that you have identified as something that you hope to be able to address through using AI. In this chapter, it is the new data that can be collected to enhance the existing data that is the focus. We will look at some of the data collection methods that might be available and the practicalities of each of these. We will describe how to undertake the data collection and we will provide links to further resources for school leaders and teachers.

DOI: 10.1201/9781003193173-4

COLLECTING EDUCATIONAL DATA

One of the challenges that many organisations face, and that we have mentioned previously, is maintaining the quality of teaching and learning when some students are learning face to face in school, some students are learning at home using technology, and the situation changes over time. It is a fundamental challenge for all teachers and leaders to ensure that no matter what the disruption, the standard of teaching and learning will remain high.

In this book, we have already thought very carefully in Chapter 3 about what it means to ask the question: what data do I need? We know that we can learn from others and that we need to think about what is relevant to the challenge we have selected. Once we have identified other works of relevance and we have identified relevant data sources, the next step is to synthesise all this data and information together. And don't forget, it is not just the data that you yourself might have collected or others in your organisation, there are sources out there that may be relevant to you that are publicly available and that can contribute to your understanding of a particular challenge.[1]

KEEP AN OPEN MIND

Many of the actions and behaviours around the complex educational challenges that we are trying to understand require broad and imaginative thinking if we are to ensure that as much of the relevant data is identified as is reasonably possible. We need this data if we are to be able to learn the important features and characteristics of a challenge. Therefore, make sure you think about what it might be relevant to collect about the people involved in the challenge you wish to understand, the physical environment and the virtual environment, the kind of resources people use. Remember also to think about whether or not there could be data about any connections that exist between the different data sources you have identified, or between these data sources and the people who are central to your challenge – the teachers and learners, for example. Make sure too that the data being identified as potentially collectable is credible.

WHAT DATA SHOULD WE COLLECT?

Back to the example of exploring how best to understand and address the challenge of maintaining the quality and continuity of teaching and learning when disruption occurs. There are a few initial key questions that need to be addressed. For example: who is going to have responsibility for collecting the data? Perhaps it will be a course or module leader, or a class teacher, a head of the department, or a teaching and learning policy lead. Secondly, we need to specify when the data is going to be collected: today, next week, next month, next year, and so forth. Plus, we need to identify over what time period the data collection will happen.

When exploring teaching and learning quality, the data is likely to be collected as soon as is reasonably possible and it should be collected over a reasonably lengthy period of time – more than a day and probably more than a week as well. The decision is likely to be dependent on many factors, including the quality and extent of the existing data sources and the practicalities of collecting new data, when people are working flat out to keep their teaching on track. We will also need to know exactly how the data is going to be collected, what format that data will take, and where it will be stored. And of course, we must be constantly mindful of the ethical implications of data collection. For example, we would need to gain permission from the people whose data we want to collect.

The pragmatics of data collection, such as the availability of people to undertake this activity, will constrain what is possible and therefore we need to be very clear about precisely what we need to find out about our selected challenge. In the example of exploring the quality of teaching and learning, we might reasonably assume for a moment that the existing data sources that can be accessed include the following:

1   The identity of all students and teachers, and the lessons and activities they are involved with
2   The outcome scores of any assessments completed

3　The type of technology and average broadband speeds that each
　　teacher and student have available to them at school and at home
4　The timetable for each day
5　Video and audio recordings of all online sessions, plus any chat

Once we have clearly specified the data we can already access, it is
more straightforward to identify what is still needed. For example,
data sources 1–4 will not be able to explain anything about the process
of teaching and learning. Data source 5 will be able to provide
data that is relevant to the process of teaching and learning, but it
may not provide much information about how the different people
who were involved felt about their experience. We can therefore
conclude that one useful additional sort of data to collect would be
data that can provide information about what teachers and learners
experienced by way of teaching and learning.

HOW CAN WE COLLECT DATA?

SURVEYS

A survey is a useful way to find out about how people have felt
about their experience of teaching and/or learning, We can also find
out what they believe they have learned, how well they believe the
system has worked, how consistent and coherent they believe their
experience has been, and how well or poorly they rate the quality
of the provision.

A survey can be described as "Information gathered by asking a
range of individuals the same questions related to their characteristics, attributes, how they live, or their opinions".[2]

There are many advantages to using a survey to collect data. For
example, you can collect data from a large number of people, which
makes this activity cost effective. If the questions and the entire survey are well designed, then the results should be reliable and credible. Detailed information can be collected if open-ended questions
are included in the survey, and if the survey is conducted online,

then the person whom we ask to complete the survey can be anonymous. Teachers and learners, or parents if children are young, could be asked to complete a survey that explores their beliefs and opinions about the nature and quality of teaching provision, for example.

TYPES OF SURVEYS

It is important to remember that designing and conducting a survey is a specialist activity. Care will need to be taken if accurate data is to be collected. One question that will need addressing is what type of survey is most suitable for the challenge being addressed. Surveys can be explanatory, which means that a survey is attempting to explain a particular phenomenon, activity, or event, for example, to explain why people behave in a particular manner.

A survey can also be descriptive, which means that it is designed to elicit from people a description, for example, of the way that a particular segment of people have behaved.

It may be that the survey needs to provide information about change over time, in which case it is referred to as a trend survey. This type of survey would need to be conducted several times in cycles to be able to provide useful and credible information about changes over time. We might, for example, decide that a survey of parents every month is a good idea during school closure when we are seeking to understand the quality and continuity of teaching provision over time. Alternatively, a snapshot approach might be sufficient; this is called a panel survey and might, for example, consist of asking parents their views about teaching provision at the end of the lockdown period. Provided of course that such an approach would provide the information required. In addition to single or multiple survey sessions, the survey itself may be designed so that the person answering the questions can do so by themselves. Alternatively, the survey might be what is called instructed, in which case a trained individual will take each participant through the survey questions, answering any clarification questions in the process.

TYPES OF SURVEY QUESTIONS

As you can see, there is a wide range of survey types and collection methods. There is also a range of types of questions and types of responses that those who are answering the survey can be asked to provide, as illustrated in Figure 4.1.

TYPES OF SURVEY ANSWERS

With respect to the types of answers that the person taking the survey can be requested to provide, the respondent could be asked to select from a set of choices or to rank a set of options. These are examples of *closed-ended answers*, or people can be asked to state their opinion about something by typing text into a blank box, which represents an *open-ended response*.

As we hope is becoming clear, a lot of thought must go into the different sorts of questions that will give us the best chance of getting the kinds of information that will really help us to understand our challenge and complement the data to which we already have access. Likewise, it is important to select the most appropriate type of survey. It is important to remember that there are people who spend their lives designing and conducting surveys and have an amazing

Types of survey questions	Key features
Factual questions	Collect systematic demographic information (that can be used to sort/filter responses).
Knowledge questions	Assess what respondents know about a particular topic and their awareness of the intervention being evaluated.
Attitudinal questions	Seek to measure respondents' opinions, beliefs, values and feelings which cannot easily be verified by through observation or external data sources.
Behavioural questions	Find out what people do (or intend to do) and how this might have changed as a consequence of the intervention.
Preference questions	Relating to different possible options and outcomes, including trade-offs between competing opportunities or actions.

Figure 4.1   Types of survey questions.

amount of expertise. This means that there is a good understanding of the kinds of mistakes that people often make when conducting surveys, from which we can learn.

COMMON SURVEY MISTAKES

Probably the most common of the mistakes made by people who are new to designing a survey is the creation of poorly worded questions. The questions may, for example, be too complex and use unfamiliar language and terminology. The questions might also be ambiguous. So, keep questions clear and simple. Avoid double negatives and double-barrelled questions. This means that it would be better to ask:

Do you believe that online teaching can be as effective as face-to-face teaching?

Than to ask:

Do you not believe that online teaching can be more ineffective than face-to-face teaching?

Similarly, it would be better to ask:

Do you feel that online teaching is alienating students from each other?

And:

Do you feel that online teaching is likely to lead to poorer social interactions in the future when face-to-face teaching is able to restart?

Than to ask:

Do you feel that online teaching is alienating students from each other because they are unable to meet and that this situation is likely to lead to poorer social interactions in the future when face-to-face teaching is able to restart?

Another mistake that is easy to make is creating biased, leading, or loaded questions. This may be because the question takes the form of a "ring true" statement or a statement that is hard to disagree with. It is also possible to word questions in a manner that is likely to lead the respondent to answer in a particular way.

Examples of this type of mistake would include asking:

> Everyone remembers their favourite teacher from school and online learning will never be able to create those memories built on significant periods of face-to-face contact.

Agree/disagree

Or to ask:

> University students are old enough to decide for themselves if they should stay on campus or go back home.

Agree/disagree

Or

> People who care about education support co-educational not single-sex schools. Which type of school would you prefer for your child?

Single sex/co-educational

Finally, it is important to avoid asking questions that are problematic for respondents. For example, questions that are offensive are clearly inappropriate. Questions that require people to recall information from memory, or assume that they know things that they may not, are also problematic, particularly if these assumptions are unnecessary. For example:

> Please state how many students attended your lectures in week 1, week 3, and week 6 of term.
>
> Please itemise the knowledge that children must learn in order for them to be able to demonstrate that they are able to write grammatical sentences in English.

For teachers, like yourself, who do not like using technology, how confident do you feel about using online teaching technology?

5 = very confident, 0 = not at all confident

All these mistakes are easily avoided once you know that they exist. Perhaps what is a little trickier is designing questions that will help you to understand your challenge in the kind of detail that is going to be useful for making decisions about how that challenge might best be tackled. The ability to do this well comes with practice, but can also be helped by working as a team. It is therefore a good idea to design questions with colleagues and to test them out on other colleagues who have not been involved in their design.

WHO IS GOING TO ANSWER THE SURVEY?

When identifying the group (known as a sample) of people whom you are going to invite to answer your survey, it is vital to be careful not to create a biased sample. We would not want, for example, to invite only a group of educators or a group of students who have only experienced one particular type of session of online learning over the last two months, to complete a survey about the different modes of instruction they have been involved with.

A NOTE ABOUT MACHINE LEARNING AND BIAS IN DATA

While we are on the subject of bias, it is important to note that bias is a significant problem when using machine learning, in particular, bias in the data set that a machine learning algorithm has processed in order to learn, that is, the training data. For example, machine learning software is being used to assist in the recruitment of staff at a large school group. This algorithm has been trained on data taken from job applications submitted by successful applicants who have joined the staff in the prior five years. There is a gender imbalance amongst the current staff with twice as many female staff as male staff. It is therefore highly likely that unless the data used to train the machine learning algorithm is adjusted so that there is data from as many male applicants as female applicants, the machine learning will be biased towards female applicants.

COLLECTING DATA THROUGH INTERVIEWS

Another method of data collection that is often used in combination with a survey is that of interviewing people. Interviewing can be useful for asking more detailed questions to small groups of respondents than is typical for a survey. Sampling is still important, because you need to ensure that the people who are interviewed can represent the population that you are focusing upon. In the same way that surveys can include closed-ended and open-ended questions, so too can interviews. However, an interview is much more like a conversation and open-ended questions are more appropriate in most instances.

TYPES OF INTERVIEWS

Interviews can be conducted face to face, online, or even by mail or email. Whatever method you are using, it is always wise to have a backup plan, particularly if you are interviewing online. The internet connection could be unreliable or unstable and then your interview would be lost.

RECORDING AND TRANSCRIBING INTERVIEWS

Recording the interview is also advisable, because it is hard to take notes without losing rapport with the interviewee and you will not remember all the answers. Audio or video recording can be used, but always test your technology ahead of time. If it uses batteries, make sure that you have spare batteries with you. Don't forget to turn on the device when you start the interview and turn it off at the end too. Finally, but most importantly, you must get the interviewee's consent to the interview before concluding it and if you are recording the interview you must store that recording in a secure location and make a backup, which is also stored in a secure location.

Once you have recorded your interviews, then you may wish to transcribe them or to use software to complete the transcription for you. For example, Otter.ai is an online software application that uses AI to transcribe audio as people are speaking. It is not 100% reliable, but it is usually good enough after a little editing, provided you have a good internet connection at the time of recording.

When transcribing or editing a transcription it is essential that you decide in advance what it is important to record. For example, is it just the content of what the interviewee says or are you interested in their pauses, silences, laughter, breathing, or other features of their behaviour? Your decision about what to transcribe should be informed by the nature of the challenge that you are exploring. Keep in mind, however, that transcribing can be a very time-consuming activity and while the result must be fit for purpose, it may not need to include absolutely every detail.

COLLECTING MULTIMODAL DATA

There are, of course, a great number of different ways in which data can be collected and it is neither possible nor appropriate to go into detail about all of them here. Our aim is to give some examples that are likely to be useful and relevant for an educational setting, so that you can try out some of the activities we discuss. However, we did say quite a lot about multimodal data in Chapter 3 and therefore we thought it useful to provide an example of how such data might be collected within a school environment.

USING A VIDEO PLATFORM TO COLLECT MULTIMODAL CLASSROOM DATA

One of the easiest and most effective ways to collect multimodal data is via video-enabled platforms, such as Iris Connect technology.[3] This type of technology allows teachers to record their lessons both class-based and online. These recordings are subsequently uploaded to each teacher's secure and private account, hosted on Iris Connect's GDPR-compliant platform. Then, at a more suitable time for the teacher, they can review and reflect upon these lessons privately or, if they wish to, share them, the control and permissions being with the individual teacher. In addition, a range of intuitive tools allow teachers to collect and analyse the data for deeper insights and to edit sections as examples of good practice.

Making connections between learning outcomes of young people becomes more apparent when we are able to observe the teaching and learning behaviours of both the teachers and the students. These observations are significant for children on an individual level, especially those with additional learning needs who may not respond in similar ways to most children, or for those children whose data shows they are stuck or have stalled in their learning.

Traditionally, this type of data has been gleaned via classroom observations, learning walks, or pupil conferences mapped against hard data. However, data collection in this way is limited. Normal classroom dynamics alter as soon as additional observers enter the classroom. Teachers feel pressured to perform or conform to set norms, and students often curtail their behaviour in the presence of senior leaders. Critical moments and, therefore, essential data points are lost as teachers try to re-engage in a process after the event.

Through video-enabled platforms, teachers can forensically focus their attention on key aspects of their teaching and lesson design, for example:

- To analyse and reflect on the language they use to organise learning and address misconceptions
- The amount and type of scaffolding they provide to individual students

- The amount of student to teacher talk
- The organisational features of the lesson and its resources

Teachers can also review the student's feedback and reactions through their:

- Responses and misconceptions
- Facial expressions
- Body language
- Voice pitch and tone
- Organisational skills
- Peer collaboration
- Self-regulation

Against this background of data collection and analysis, teachers can review and reflect on the extent to which classroom factors supported or hindered learning progress. Collecting multimodal data in this way leads to more authentic data-led discussions.

AN EXAMPLE: EXPLORING THE GENDER GAP

Back in Chapter 3, one of the examples that we provided was that of the performance gender gap between boys and girls or male and female students. As we noted, this is a recurring issue that draws the attention of school leaders and staff at all levels. The gender gap may be associated with a particular subject area such as maths. We will use this as an example to work with here to identify the sorts of data that might already exist and that might be collected in this instance. Throughout the example, we identify the activities we have discussed in this book so far with the steps in the AI Readiness training programme.

Imagine, for example, that the question, or the particular fact, of the gender gap challenge that we have decided to focus upon is: identifying and exploring the features of the gender gap for maths in key stage 2 within English primary schools.

CHALLENGE SELECTED IN STEP 2
OF THE AI READINESS PROCESS

The gender gap for maths in key stage 2 within an English primary school

In particular, what are the features of this gap – in other words, at this stage we want to explore it and see what we can find out.

STEP 3 – DATA THAT EXISTS
AND CAN BE ACCESSED

The curriculum for students of this age and the outcomes of students for the past five years – stored in the cloud and on the video platform server:

- Education attainment outcomes including standardised tests, cognitive tests, and curriculum tests (e.g., schools assessments or national tests or examinations)
- Comparisons of special educational needs data and second language data between boys and girls
- Data on attendance and exclusion for boys and girls since joining the school (looking at gaps in teaching and learning)
- The quality of teaching provision demonstrated by observation, CPD needs, 360 peer reviews, and lesson plans and book moderation, including appropriate levels of challenge (a range of strategies rather than procedural tasks that children routinely carry out), pupil groupings, and collaborations
- Effective feedback as evidenced by book moderations, observations, pupil conferences, video
- Notes about teachers' perceptions of their learners' outcomes – stored on the school server
- Data about setting/not setting, numbers of learners in a class, the ratio of boys to girls stored on the school server
- Reports about student's readiness to learn – mindset/confidence levels compared to outcomes – collected via a survey and stored on the school server

- Parental perceptions of maths and their own ability in this subject – collected via a survey and stored on the school server
- There may also be access to behaviour logs, homework records, reading age records
- Resources used and quality/level of differentiation to meet the needs of the students

STEP 4 – DATA TO BE COLLECTED

Learning behaviour data, such as social cues, facial or body language, voice pitch and tone, poor organisational skills, personal space and boundaries collected via the classroom video capture system and stored on the video system platform to enable use to evidence:

- The amount of teacher talk compared to student talk
- Engagement in learning activities with time given to internalise activities and apply strategies
- Teachers' lesson delivery including language used, responses to misconceptions and scaffolding, and worked examples used to enable students to analyse different strategies
- Discussion/collaboration between peers
- Pupils' use of visual representation to aid understanding as recorded in work books

In this chapter, we have explored the process of data collection in the context of a challenge that has been identified as important. Data collection needs to be designed carefully and must complement that data which is already available, as discussed in Chapter 3. This chapter encompasses the necessary information to complete Step 4 of the AI Readiness process. In Chapter 5, we will explain how all the data you have accumulated for your selected challenge, as discussed in Chapters 3 and 4, can be prepared and processed using machine learning AI tools and techniques, to reveal useful information.

USEFUL RESOURCES

Institute for Education Sciences: What Works Clearinghouse (https://ies.ed.gov /ncee/wwc); *VIDEO TOUR (https://ies.ed.gov/ncee/wwc/multimedia/27)*

Johns Hopkins University – Best Evidence Encyclopaedia (http://www.beste-vidence.org)

Education Endowment Foundation (https://educationendowmentfoundation .org.uk/evidence-summaries/teaching-learning-toolkit)

EDUCAUSE – Higher Education (https://www.educause.edu/ecar/research -publications)

Google Scholar https://scholar.google.co.uk/

IRIS Connect: Developing classroom dialogue and feedback through collective video reflection: https://educationendowmentfoundation.org.uk/projects -and-evaluation/projects/iris-connect

Investing in Video Professional Learning | A Guide | IRIS Connect

Visible Learning for Teachers: Maximizing Impact on Learning John Hattie: https://www.routledge.com/Visible-Learning-for-Teachers-Maximizing -Impact-on-Learning/Hattie/p/book/9780415690157

FFT Aspire: https://fftaspire.org. The leading reporting and data tool for schools, local authorities, and academy chains.

Nesta: Making the most of data. https://media.nesta.org.uk/documents/ Making_the_most_of_data_in_schools_

2017, 7th ed London: Routledge.

Research methods in education, 7th edition – Academia.edu

https://www.academia.edu › Research_Methods_in_Edu...

Zina O'Leary. (2021). The Essential Guide to Doing Your Research Project - 4th ed. SAGE Publications.

M. Denscombe. (2017). *The good research guide: For small-scale social research projects.* (UK Higher Education, OUP Humanities and Social Science Studies)

6th ed. McGraw-Hill Education.

NOTES

1 And don't forget, it is not just the data that you yourself might have collected or others in your organisation, there are sources out there that may be relevant to you that are publicly available, and that can contribute to

your understanding of a particular challenge. See, for example, https://openknowledgemaps.org/ andhttp://researchmap.digitalpromise.org/

2 "Information gathered by asking a range of individuals the same questions related to their characteristics, attributes, how they live, or their opinions." Cite source

3 Iris technology Iris Connect (Classroom Video Technology) https://www.irisconnect.com/uk/products-and-services/video-technology-for-teachers

5

APPLYING AI TO
UNDERSTAND DATA

This chapter is all about applying AI techniques to data, the sort of data that we discussed in Chapters 3 and 4. Data about a challenge that your particular school or college is facing and that you hope AI might be able to help you solve.

So far, we have tried to enthuse you about AI, so that you might also enthuse your colleagues and peers to feel that AI is something that would be of benefit. We have introduced you to old-fashioned AI based on rules GOFAI. This was AI that could not learn and improve. Nevertheless, it still achieved some pretty sophisticated and very useful things. We have also discussed modern AI, which is mostly machine learning, which is AI that can learn.

For example, a teacher, who is working with a class of students using an AI platform that uses machine learning to adapt the instruction that it provides for each of their pupils, according to that pupil's needs. The more that this platform interacts with students, the better it will get at adapting, because it will learn more about the students, and more about how to adapt to the needs of each particular student, or a lecturer using some AI software that applies machine learning to look for examples of plagiarism. Again, the more examples of plagiarism that the software processes, the more it learns to recognise examples of plagiarism.

DOI: 10.1201/9781003193173-5

AI uses many different sorts of techniques, including many different types of machine learning. In this chapter, we will be talking about a type of *classical* machine learning called *unsupervised machine learning* and how it can be applied to educational data in order to help us understand that data.

TYPES OF MACHINE LEARNING

Machine learning can broadly be classified into *unsupervised machine learning* and *supervised machine learning*. Within these different categories of machine learning, there are yet more different types and different sorts of techniques. Increasingly, people become specialists in a particular technique or a particular category of techniques, and you certainly do not need to know about all of them.

The aim of this book is to help you understand the kinds of things that AI can do. The reason for talking through the application of one type of machine learning in this chapter is to help you understand what the AI is doing by metaphorically *getting inside the algorithm*, as it were (see Figure 5.1).

Figure 5.1 Opening up "the black box" of machine learning.

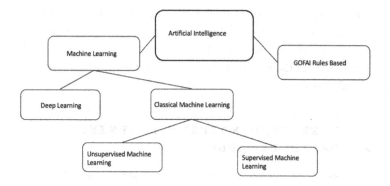

Figure 5.2 Types of AI.

We aim to unpack what AI can do with the sorts of data that you might be interested in processing. Hopefully, this approach will help you to understand how AI techniques can help you to better understand your data and your challenge. With this increased understanding, then, you should be able to better select the kind of AI that you are going to use in order to address one or some of the challenges you face. Figure 5.2 illustrates some of the different types of AI.

UNSUPERVISED MACHINE LEARNING

So far our discussions about machine learning AI have actually described supervised machine learning. This is the type of machine learning that is used when you want to train the machine learning to be able to find something specific in the data that it processes: a traffic light, a staircase, a child's face, a particular grade of exam script, for example. However, we do not always know exactly what we want machine learning to find in the data, so we need another type of machine learning that can find patterns in the data we present to it for processing.

Unsupervised machine learning is the tool we use in a situation where we *do not know what we are looking for in the data* and so we cannot get the machine learning algorithm to learn what the target data we want to find looks like, so that it can find further examples of this target data in the data set that we provide to the machine learning algorithm for it to process. Rather, the unsupervised machine learning algorithm explores the data to look for patterns. It searches for similarities in the data that might tell us something that we do not already know.

UNSUPERVISED MACHINE LEARNING: A WORKED EXAMPLE

In the previous chapters we have used an example of a challenge that educators are facing that can be framed into a question:

> How can we know that the quality of teaching and learning is maintained when moving from face-to-face to mainly online provision?

We will continue to use this example in this chapter as we work through the steps involved in applying AI to the data that we have accessed and collated (as described in Chapter 3) and collected (as described in Chapter 4). Using an example like this necessitates a good deal of simplification. A good analogy can be seen in our own brain's activity. At the neuronal level, there can be lots of ingredients that go into a decision that is either a clear "yes" or "no" decision. Perhaps the decision is a very basic subconscious decision about putting one foot in front of the other when walking. There will be a vast array of contextual information we will be processing, such as the incline of the ground, the weather conditions, the evenness of the surface, etc. In the end, however, all these ingredients are simplified into that "yes" or "no" decision – to take a step or not. In the same way, as we discuss the teaching and learning example, we will lose much of the complexity in order to simplify it and enable you to see things more clearly.

As always, as we work through this example, it is important to bear in mind the sorts of activities that AI is good at, better than us, in many senses. Plus, the sorts of things that we humans can do better than AI. As we progress through this book and increase our understanding of AI, we want to make sure that we think about applying AI to tasks that are best done by AI. And that we maintain the use of our human intelligence for the tasks that we still do way better than any form of AI.

Back to:

> *How can we know that the quality of teaching and learning is maintained when moving from face-to-face to mainly online provision?*

The data to which we might already have access could, for example, include:

- Data from interactions that students have as they are learning online: log data from interactions with technology, including button clicks and mouse movements.
- Conversations between students: perhaps these are conversations that happen in breakout rooms in an online platform, or perhaps they are conversations that happen face to face because some of the students are receiving some face-to-face teaching at school.
- Performance data from tests, exams, and other assessments.
- Some recorded interviews, perhaps about one of the problems that students have been asked to solve. Students have been asked to interview each other about the progress they are making in the problem-solving activity.
- We may also have recordings of students and of staff when they were interviewed when joining the organisation.
- We might also be able to access some eye tracking data from video data captured as students learn online or through the use of a classroom video platform for those students who are in the classroom. This data may show us if students are looking at the camera, looking at their assignment, or looking at something or someone else.
- To add to this existing data, we have also decided to conduct a survey to find out about how people feel about the teaching they have been doing (teacher survey), and about the learning

in which they have engaged (student survey). We are also asking everyone about their past experience with technology, their confidence in their ability to use the online technology effectively, etc.

There will be a whole host of distinct types of data available to use, and it will have different characteristics. For example, some of the data could be captured over the last few weeks, and some data could be more historical. Some data might be incomplete. Some might be quantitative, whilst other data might be qualitative. We therefore need to prepare our data, so that we can apply AI techniques to the data to understand more about our challenge.

MACHINE LEARNING AS COOKING

I find it helpful to think about this situation as being a bit like cooking. There are many types of cooking. We can bake, we can fry, we can broil, boil, or braise. We can grill, we can poach, we can smoke, sear, or sous vide. Just for a moment imagine that you are part of one of those TV shows where you are presented with a set of ingredients that are placed on a table and hidden under a cloth. You pull back the cloth to reveal the ingredients from which you must make something wonderful. Your instructions state that you are to make a dessert and that you must use all the ingredients in making your dessert. Think about the ingredients as being a little bit like the data to which we want to apply AI. Back to the table. You have just whipped off the cloth covering the ingredients in our imaginary cooking show. You have eggs, and you have raspberries, plus there is cream and sugar.

What type of cooking method would be best applied to these ingredients? Frying is not an option, because whilst we could fry an egg, we have to use all the ingredients not just eggs. Grilling also looks unlikely to be suitable. Similarly, broiling or boiling is not really appropriate, but maybe baking could work for this.

The same type of situation exists when it comes to applying AI to our data "ingredients"; we need to decide what sort of AI could and should be applied. This decision is largely driven by the ingredients available and the challenge that we need to address, just as it is with cooking. There may be several options available to us for the same set of ingredients. Experience will help us to know which option to try first. Fortunately, unlike food, data can be subjected to multiple AI techniques that are appropriate to the type of data and the challenge being addressed.

Back to the cooking ingredients. We know we are required to solve the challenge of creating a dessert from the ingredients available. We also know that baking is likely to be the most appropriate cooking method to apply. The options available are now constrained by these parameters, but there are still options. Should we make raspberry pavlova or should we make raspberry souffle? Which of these is going to best meet the requirements of the cooking show, the challenge? We decide on raspberry souffle, because we have more experience of making this and therefore believe that a good result is more likely than with pavlova. Now this choice has been made, we know the method that we need to complete in order to produce the solution to our challenge: a dessert using the ingredients available to us.

The situation with data and applying AI is not so dissimilar. We have looked at our data (the ingredients) and the challenge (exploring the quality of teaching and learning when moving some provision online). We decide that the most suitable type of AI (cf. type of cooking) to be applied to these ingredients and this challenge is machine learning (cf. baking). Finally, we make a choice about the type of result we want to produce: finding patterns in the data for the teaching and learning interactions that have happened online and face to face (cf. pavlova or souffle). We can therefore now also choose the method of machine learning that we are going to apply; we choose unsupervised machine learning.

Returning for a moment to the raspberry souffle situation. We are now faced with needing to go through a set of preparations to be able to apply the baking process to the ingredients and produce a souffle. First, we have to wash the raspberries. Then we have to crack the eggs and whisk them. And then we have to add the sugar into the whisked eggs. We also have to whip up the cream and add that to the beaten eggs and the sugar. Finally, we add the washed raspberries. Then we need to mix it all together in the bowl. We now have the souffle mix and just need to put the mix into a dish, or a set of individual portion dishes, and we will be ready to apply the cooking method of baking to the prepared ingredients. As you can see, there is a lot of preparation. In fact, it may take longer to do all that preparation than it does to bake the souffle, which is really quick to bake.

For our education data and educational challenge situation, we want to explore the extent to which we have maintained the quality of teaching and learning, as things have moved online. It is important to note that there are many ways in which we could analyse our data, many of which have nothing to do with AI, but the point here is to see what extra insights and understanding the use of AI techniques can bring to the kind of analysis that is normally done with educational data. In our example here, we also want to understand more about AI.

PREPARING THE DATA (THE INGREDIENTS)

Back to our data, the ingredients that we need to prepare and process. We have the following data:

- Audio recordings: from conversations between students. Perhaps these are conversations that happen in breakout rooms in an online platform, or perhaps they are conversations that happen face to face because some of the students are receiving some face-to-face teaching at school.
- Numerical data: from assessments of various types and quantities – from tests, exams, and other assessments.
- Video data: students have been asked to interview each other about the progress they are making in a problem-solving activity. We also have some recordings of students and of staff from their interviews when joining the organisation.

- Log data from interactions that students have as they are learning online, including button clicks and mouse movements.
- Eye tracking data about the direction of each student's eye gaze, captured as students learn online, or through the use of a classroom video platform for those students who are in the classroom. This data shows us if students are looking at the camera, looking at their assignment, or looking at something or someone else.
- Survey response data: about how people feel about the teaching they have been doing (teacher survey), and about the learning in which they have engaged (student survey). We also have information about everyone's past experience with technology, and their confidence in their ability to use the online technology effectively (Figure 5.3). It may be that not all the data that you prepare will be used for machine learning analysis; some data sources might be analysed using different methods. This can be useful, as we shall see in Chapter 6, when we compare the results from the machine learning analysis with findings from the survey that were not analysed with machine learning, but with more traditional analytical methods that do not involve AI.

The ingredients: the data we have collated and collected

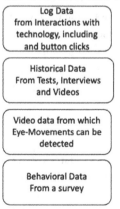

Figure 5.3 The data "ingredients" for analysis.

We now need to think about how we prepare these ingredients, how we clean them, and how we combine them together to produce an outcome. In this instance it is not a raspberry souffle, it is an increased understanding of the challenge that we chose and of what AI is and how it works.

Initially, when we start off with our data, we have to do something similar to the process of washing the raspberries, whisking the eggs, whipping the cream, and mixing the ingredients together that we did for the raspberry souffle. Let us think about this in terms of workflow. We have our six different types of data and we need to prepare them. We now need to clean them, we need to organise them, and we need to transform them into a consistent data set.

CLEANING THE DATA

Don't worry, we are not going to get water on our data and clean it up like that, but what we are going to try to make it uniform, try to make it look neat and nice and easy to work with. So why do we do this? Because we need very high-quality data, that is accurate, that is as complete as it can possibly be, that is consistent and that is uniform. It is also important to remember that there is never anything that you can call *raw data*. Raw data does not exist, because all data is collected for a reason. Somebody, somewhere has made a decision to collect that data, or for that data to be collected whilst other activities are going on. There is always a context for that data, that is usually lost when it is extracted from the context of its creation. There is always added information to any data that includes contextual information that is super important and that we need to try and capture in some way.

As we clean and prepare the data, we need to remove errors and look for impossible values that will be incorrect values. There are always mistakes in data, so we have to go through it carefully to check that they have all been removed. We also need to look for duplicate entries and irrelevant data. We need to decide what to do about *outliers* in the data.

Outliers are values that are vastly different from most of the values in a data set. We need to think carefully about what we do, and usually we remove the outliers. However, we need to try and avoid removing too many outliers and reducing all our values to the average. Once a decision has been made about outliers, then we must make sure that we apply the decision consistently to all the parts of the data.

ORGANISING AND INTEGRATING THE DATA

Different data sets often have different labelling methods. We might, for example, have student gender in one data set described as *female* or *male*, and in another data set it is described as *girl and boy*. We must ensure that all the labels use the same conventions, so that they are recognised as being the same thing by the algorithm, because, for example, the algorithm will not know that the label "female" means the same as the label "girl".

In order to build credibility into our data set, we need to take precise actions with our data, always aiming for quality and always documenting as we go, so that others can know the approach that we have adopted. This is important; for example, if the processing done by the AI we apply does not behave in the way we would expect and we need to go back and look at the documentation to see if there was anything about the approach that we used in preparing the data that could have been done better.

The way we prepare the data depends upon the type of data. In the same way that hoovering a carpet to clean it is not the same as washing a window, and in our baking analogy we wash the raspberries, but not the eggs. We crack the eggs and not the cream. This cleaning and preparing process is extremely important and involves a lot of work. This phase of the process of applying AI is likely to account for 80% of the time involved in applying AI to data (Figure 5.4).

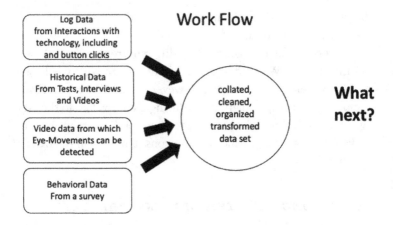

Figure 5.4 The workflow after the cleaning and preparation work.

FEATURE ENGINEERING

Once we have done all the collation cleaning, preparation, and integrating of our data, the next step in the workflow is to think about the patterns that the AI will identify in the data and the features these patterns will be based upon. For example, the feature of low confidence with technology might be grouped with the feature of poor performance in assessments and the feature of low student activity (as represented in the interaction logs). Feature engineering is the process that we now perform with the data. This process is a great example of Artificial and human intelligences working together.

The application of AI could identify hundreds of features in the data, which will not lead to helpful information. Therefore, human expertise can help by suggesting features that could be relevant. For example, being active is important for students and therefore a feature of importance that you want to explore in your data is the number of actions completed by every student. This can be described as a *simple feature*. In addition, you and your colleagues as the educational experts might also decide that the proportion of sessions that each teacher leads in the first five hours of their working day are often more effective and therefore a feature that is: the proportion of sessions by educator N that take place in the first five hours of their day could be appropriate and useful. This type of feature is more complex than the previous simple example and is referred to as *an engineered or derived feature*.

Despite taking time to identify features that could be important in explaining the data patterns that the AI identifies, we still have too many features. We need to reduce the number of features, or dimensions as they are often called, and identify a small set of dimensions that accounts for most of the differences between the different sorts of teaching and learning interaction represented in the data (Figure 5.5).

PRINCIPAL COMPONENT ANALYSIS

There is a technique that can be used as part of the unsupervised machine learning process that will help us with this task. This technique is called *principal component analysis (PCA)*. As the name suggests, this technique is about identifying the main, or *principal*, components that account for the variation between patterns in the data.

In our example, the patterns in the data represent the different styles of teaching and learning sessions that are described by

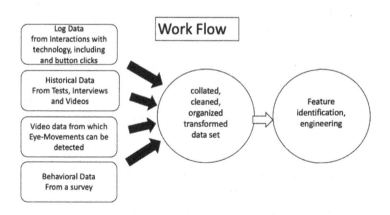

Figure 5.5 The workflow after feature engineering.

the data that the machine learning is processing. If we are able to identify a small number of features that explain the majority of the variation between these session styles, then we can start to understand more about the sort of teaching and learning that has been happening. This can be the first step in helping us to determine whether or not quality in teaching and learning has been maintained.

The PCA process of identifying the principal components will produce a set of components (features) that explain a certain percentage of the variation between the patterns in the data.

Say, for example, that in our data set about teaching and learning quality and standards, there are 85 different sorts of features. We want to identify a set of four or five features that explain most of the variation; we will never identify a set of features that explains 100% of the variation, because there will always be anomalies. We need to aim for as high a percentage as possible.

So, we run our machine learning principal component analysis and identify five dimensions that account for a high percentage of the variation between the types of teaching and learning sessions for which we have data. The five features are:

1   The average amount of student activity as shown in their log data
2   The geographic location of the student, where are they – in home or in school
3   The style of interaction – whole group or small group collaboration
4   The use of technology – just the online platform, or online platform and some other additional technology as well
5   The average age of the educator

As educational experts, we might look at this set of features or dimensions and decide that the average age of the educator is not likely to be relevant. We therefore challenge dimension five, and it is removed with little loss in the overall accuracy. With only four dimensions, once the average age of the educator has been removed, the remaining dimensions explain 82% of the variation, as compared with 85% when the five dimensions were used.

We have now identified four features that we can explore in lots of different ways. Because these four features account for a high percentage of the differences between the different sorts of interactions that happened when most teaching and learning were done online.

CLUSTER ANALYSIS

What can we now do with this finding: the identification of four dimensions (features) that explain 82% of the variation in our data set?

We apply another unsupervised machine learning technique from our AI toolkit:

cluster analysis. This is the point at which we use machine learning to find clusters or patterns within the data that relate to those four features that we have identified through principal component analysis. The patterns identified through the application of cluster analysis will be based on those four dimensions. This is unsupervised machine learning and we are looking to identify natural groupings, or patterns, in the data.

Figure 5.6 illustrates the types of AI shown in Figure 5.2, with the addition of feature engineering and PCA (Figure 5.7).

In our example about the quality of teaching and learning, it may be that the natural groupings indicate that there are four different clusters or profiles. The profiles are illustrated in Figure 5.8. In Profile 1, the values that were found to form the profile (pattern) are:

1   Average numbers of actions by students.
2   Just above average sessions in school.
3   Sessions are more likely to be just online.
4   Sessions are more likely to be with the whole class, rather than small groups.

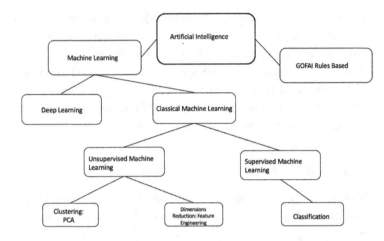

Figure 5.6 Types of AI, version 2 with dimension reduction and clustering added.

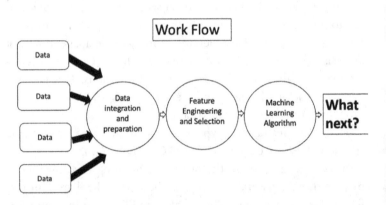

Figure 5.7 The workflow after PCA has been completed.

Profile 2 is quite different. The values in this profile are:

1 High for learning at home
2 Slightly above-average activity by students
3 Higher use of additional technology, as well as the online technology

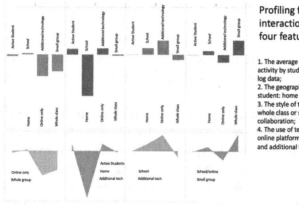

Profiling four types of interaction, using four features

1. The average amount of online activity by students as show in the log data;
2. The geographic location of the student: home or school;
3. The style of the interaction: whole class or small group collaboration;
4. The use of technology: just the online platform or online platform and additional technology;

Figure 5.8 The profiles that can be extracted using PCA.

Profile 3 has the distinguishing features of:

1 A high value for the use of additional technology
2 A higher-than-average value for the learning location being at school
3 Slightly more whole classroom sessions than small group sessions

Finally, Profile 4:

1 Has higher-than-average value for small group sessions
2 Is more likely than not to involve the use of some additional technology as well as the online platform

It is interesting to be able to identify the different styles of interactions that are represented in the data about teaching and learning. However, this is just the start, because there is a lot more we can find out, as you will see in Chapter 6.

We have covered a lot of ground in this chapter and we hope that you have found it understandable, interesting, and useful. We have used an example challenge to introduce you to the processes that are involved when we apply *unsupervised machine learning* to educational data in order to help us understand that data:

> *How can we know that the quality of teaching and learning is maintained when moving from face-to-face to mainly online provision?*

We have discussed the fact that before any machine learning algorithm can be let loose on our data, that data must be cleaned and prepared. We used a cooking analogy to explain the different steps. We have also described feature engineering and principal component analysis as machine learning tools that we can use to explore complex data. These tools allow us to identify ways of reducing the complexity of the data, through the identification of key features, or dimensions, that enable data to be grouped together into a small set of profiles.

The results from the application of unsupervised machine learning tools to the data that we suggested for exploring the quality of teaching and learning when moving from face-to-face to mainly online provision are not based on us actually processing the data sources we identify. The results are, however, based on real data from an educational setting that we have analysed using exactly the AI tools that we describe here. That real data included much the same types of data as those described here. It is a very realistic example, but it is not a case study.

Well done, you now have Step 5 in the AI Readiness process under your belt. In the next chapter, we will discuss what more we can learn from the results of applying unsupervised machine learning to a data set. This will involve some use of supervised machine learning and revisiting GOFAI.

6

LEARNING FROM AI

This chapter is all about what we can learn from analysing the data that we have collated using AI tools and techniques. This is an exciting stage in the process and a wonderful way to understand more about AI.

As we discussed in Chapter 5, there are many different types or methods of AI. As with cooking, the choice of method is influenced by the type of data that we wish to process and the kind of outcome we hope to achieve. So, in the same way that the sorts of ingredients that we use when cooking and the sort of dish we wish to produce influence the cooking method we choose, so too the data sources and the purpose of applying the AI influence the choice of AI.

The purpose for applying AI can be described as the *imperative* of AI. Not only do we need to select the AI method, but we also need to do a lot of cleaning and preparing of the data that we have collated and collected for it to be processed by our selected AI method. This cleaning and preparation phase is time consuming but important.

The purpose of this book is not to teach you how to select the most appropriate AI method or to show you how to clean and prepare the data. The purpose of introducing and discussing these issues – the selection of AI method and the cleaning and preparing of data – is to make you aware that these choices and activities need to be completed before an AI can be applied to any data.

DOI: 10.1201/9781003193173-6

We are going to return to the example challenge that we have discussed in previous chapters:

> How can we know that the quality of teaching and learning is maintained when moving from face-to-face to mainly online provision?

TO RECAP

In Chapter 5, we identified some data sources and once cleaned and prepared we used the example of applying unsupervised machine learning to the data to show you what the data could tell us about our challenge. Not only that, we also wanted to show you what happens when unsupervised machine learning is applied to data to help you understand more about machine learning AI and its potential. Remember too that the application of unsupervised machine learning had the purpose of finding patterns in the data we had prepared. We then went through the process of feature identification and feature reduction to identify a small set of features that would account for most of the variance in the data – that is, the variations between the teaching and learning sessions for which we had data. In our example, we identified four features in our data that accounted for 82% of the variations in the data. Please see Figure 6.1 for the workflow that we discussed in Chapter 5.

Once we had identified these four features, we were able to use a clustering technique to identify four different teaching and learning session types/categories or profiles.

WHAT WE CAN LEARN FROM THE RELATIONSHIPS BETWEEN DIFFERENT DATA SOURCES?

A question that we can now usefully ask about our data is: could the patterns in the data that produced the four clusters or profiles relate to other data, and could this tell us more about the quality of teaching and learning in face-to-face to online provision? For example, could

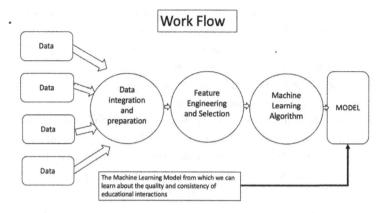

Figure 6.1 The workflow that has enabled us to explore the teaching session profiles.

the profiles relate to data from the survey that we conducted that told us about things like confidence levels, amongst students and staff? Could there be a difference in the confidence levels of students in the different profiles, and, if so, what might that mean for the suitability of this type of interaction for particular sorts of students?

We know the relationship between the survey data and the profiles is not a causal one. It is not that confidence levels cause particular profiles but a relationship between the confidence level of the students and the nature of the profile they belong to might provide further insights.

Imagine the situation where the level of student confidence is shown to be related to or to *correlate to* the type of teaching session they experienced. You will recall that each of the four profiles represents a different type of teaching session. Could it be that students who reported low levels of confidence were more likely to have participated in a Profile 1 teaching session where learning was mainly online, and mainly in whole group sessions? Is either of these features something that perhaps has an impact on students' confidence? We don't know, but having identified this relationship, we could explore that question specifically if we wanted to.

Perhaps the processed data also illustrates that much higher levels of confidence were reported by students who were not just using technology to learn online, also some additional technology as part of their teaching session. This would point us towards exploring more about what that additional technology was and how it was used in the teaching sessions (Figure 6.2).

There is much to be learned from exploring the different relationships between the profiles produced by the application of the *unsupervised machine learning algorithm* and some of the other data that we have. Imagine how these examples, and other examples like these, proceed to indicate how we might start to address:

> *How can we know that the quality of teaching and learning is maintained when moving from face-to-face to mainly online provision?*

Not only can we look for relationships between the data from the survey and the teaching session profiles, but we can also look for relationships between other data sources and the profiles. For example, eye tracking data. You may recall that eye tracking data is a

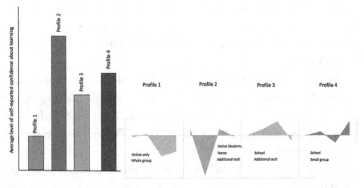

For example data from the survey about student confidence?

Figure 6.2   The relationships between the profiles and the data about confidence.

For example data from the survey about student confidence

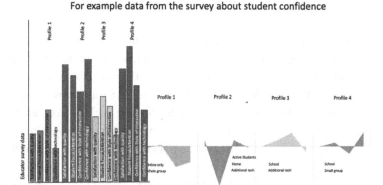

Figure 6.3 Comparing the profiles with several aspects of the survey data.

valuable type of multimodal data that we discussed in Chapter 3 (Figure 6.3).

LEARNING ABOUT COLLABORATIVE PROBLEM-SOLVING FROM EYE TRACKING DATA

You may recall that in Chapter 3 we discussed the way in which existing research can help us to know what type of data might be useful. Specifically, we used the example of findings from psychology about the correlation between the synchrony of the way that students were looking when they working together, and their proficiency at collaborative problem-solving (CPS). In other words, the researchers found a *correlation* between effective CPS and students' eye gaze synchrony.

We will use a case study example, which is based on research completed with colleagues a few years ago. There is a link at the end of this chapter that will take you to more information about this research if you wish to know more. Whilst you read this research case study, try to keep in mind the example challenge we have been focusing upon and think about how similar approaches to those we describe might be used to help us explore the quality of teaching and learning sessions.

In our research, groups of three school students were set the task of working together to develop an interactive toy. As they worked to tackle this task, they had to work together to solve a range of problems. We collected a range of different data sources as the students worked together, including video footage of their faces. From this video we were able to detect when students were looking at any point in their CPS activity. Eye tracking technology could have been used to achieve the same result, but it is not always available. Additionally, a question that has been asked by teachers at some of our talks about AI Readiness is:

> How does the video data become data that can be used by a machine learning algorithm?

We therefore thought it useful to explain this process. One way to transform the video data from a stream of images and sounds to something numerical is by "hand coding". This process involves researchers watching the video stream overlaid with the eye tracking data (see Figure 6.1 for an illustration of this situation). Each of the three students is allocated an identifier: student A, student B, student C. Researchers watch the video and they enter values into a spreadsheet for what each student is doing at regular intervals: the value X, when any of the three students is looking at the screen showing the problem the students are trying to solve; the value AB, when student A is looking at student B; the value AC, when student A is looking at student C; the value BA, when student B is looking at student A; the value BC, when student B is looking at student C; and so on. These numbers in the spreadsheet can now be used for processing, once they have been cleaned and prepared of course. This hand-coding process is time consuming and could be automated if required. However, it provides a useful example of how video can be converted into the sort of data that can be processed. In fact, we did subsequently apply machine learning to analyse data from eye tracking software automatically.

When we analysed the data about student eye gaze synchrony and compared the data with the findings from an independent expert who had viewed the video footage, we were able to identify points at which each of the groups was or was not collaborating effectively to solve the problem. The comparison revealed a correlation between synchrony of eye gaze and effective CPS.[1]

In wanting to explore the quality of teaching and learning across face-to-face and online teaching, we could think about using eye tracking data as follows, for example. We could investigate the teaching session profiles that included group work where eye tracking data was available and see if there are any relationships between student synchrony and student confidence, or indeed teacher confidence. Or we could explore whether students who were working alone and who were continually looking at the screen were also more active, or more confident, for example.

SUPERVISED MACHINE LEARNING

Having looked at unsupervised learning, we are now going to look at supervised learning, and in particular, we are going to look at the process of classification. Classification is a problem traditionally tackled using supervised machine learning. Remember supervised machine learning is used when we know what we are looking for. We previously used unsupervised learning, because we did not know what we were looking for and were interested in what patterns existed in the data.

Another cooking analogy: in the same way that when you are making a cake, there are different ways in which you can combine your ingredients. For example, you can rub the fat into the flour using the "rubbing in" method, or you can melt the fat with the sugar using the "melting" method, or you can beat the fat with the sugar until they are light and fluffy using the "creaming" method. Your choice of method for mixing up the ingredients will depend upon the type of cake you wish to make. A Victoria sandwich is best made with the creaming method, but gingerbread requires the melting method.

The same is true with classification; there are different methods or algorithms that are used as part of the classification process, and the choice of algorithm will make a difference to the output. Therefore, the choice of algorithm depends on what you are trying to achieve and the sorts of data that you are processing. Remember, however, that the purpose of this book is not to teach you how to select the most appropriate AI technique; it is to introduce you to the basic principles and to make you aware of the choices and activities that need to be completed when applying AI to data.

Think about the data for our example challenge. In Chapter 5 we described four-session profiles that resulted from using unsupervised machine learning. We also looked at individual data sets to explore the existence of a relationship between teaching session style and factors such as student confidence, teacher confidence, and student activity levels. We can now think about the different aspects of the data available to us and any of the associations between a data element, such as student confidence, and teaching session style. Perhaps it would also be useful to be able to predict, for example, in which styles of teaching session might particular types of students be most likely to thrive? Or, to predict the styles of teaching session that each teacher might most enjoy and be best at delivering.

We could train a supervised machine learning to recognise the types of students and the style of sessions in which they thrive, or to recognise which style of teaching suits different types of teachers. It would then be possible to use supervised machine learning to process data about types of students in order to predict the style of a teaching session in which they would thrive. It must be noted that many, many data cases evidencing student types prospering well in particular teaching session styles would be required to train such a supervised machine learning algorithm, and we probably do not have access to a large enough data sample. However, we hope that this example has illustrated the ways in which a supervised machine learning could be applied.

We also hope that you are starting to understand the types of useful information that AI methods, such as machine learning, can produce by processing educational data sets. So far, machine learning has been the AI tool under discussion, but it is also valuable to consider what some of those Good Old-Fashioned AI (GOFAI) approaches can contribute to help us better understand the challenges we face.

We have already discussed the way that supervised machine learning could be used to make predictions. In our example challenge, we suggested that this AI tool could be used, for example, to predict the kinds of students or teachers who might be likely to do well or not to do well in particular styles of teaching sessions, as indicated by the profiles we extracted from the data using unsupervised machine learning. Remember, as we take the next step, that the aim here is to explain the way in which AI can be helpful for you to better understand the challenges you face AND to help you better understand what AI is and what it can do.

What this book aims to achieve is that once you understand more about AI and about the challenges you have identified, then you will be in a much better position to decide how you might use AI to tackle those challenges. This book is taking you through the process of AI application, helping you to "get inside" machine learning algorithms, as it were, and to understand the power of the data that you have available to you.

Back to Good Old-Fashioned AI (GOFAI), remember Chapter 1? Much of GOFAI is based on the idea of using rules to make a decision, for example, about a medical diagnosis, or what support to provide for a learner who is struggling to solve a mathematics problem.

The rules that underpin these rule-based AI systems take the form of IF/THEN statements. For example,

> IF student N has failed to reverse the numerator and denominator of Fraction X, THEN play "finding the reciprocal" video, AND complete finding the reciprocal for Fraction n, AND move student to next action, AND play "motivational video n".

In the same way that we turned to the experts to help us identify potential features of interest when we first applied unsupervised machine learning to the educational data in Chapter 5, this GOFAI example will require experts to construct the rules. In both AI methods, humans are involved at different points, although the nature of the division of labour between Artificial and human intelligence is different for each AI method. Nevertheless, there is always a relationship between human and artificial intelligence.

Let's step back to our core example challenge:

> How can we know that the quality of teaching and learning is maintained when moving from face to face to mainly online provision?

A rule-based system could be useful, for example, after the unsupervised learning has processed the data and we have identified a set of different teaching session styles. At this point we might have concerns about students who have particular stresses, strains, troubles, or issues that they need to tackle. This might be depression or anxiety or lack of confidence, for example.

We would like to make sure that the students about whom we have concerns are directed towards teaching sessions that are more likely to be suitable for their needs. Perhaps small group work suits them particularly well.

As we look towards the future and the way that we might use a mix of online and face-to-face teaching, we may decide that a rule-based system could be helpful when timetabling sessions for particular groups of students.

Alternatively, a rule-based system might be designed to provide feedback to teachers as students engage in collaborative problem-solving. Recall, eye tracking can be used to capture the direction in which a student is looking, and from this we can identify whether a group of students are synchronised in their gaze. Being synchronised in this way gives us a small clue about the effectiveness with which these students are working together. Imagine that we have another dozen small clues from our data analysis, then we might create a rule-based system that uses this information to send different sorts of feedback to the teacher to help them optimise the support that they provide for each group of students.

In this chapter, we have discussed the manner in which we can learn extremely useful information about an educational challenge through the application of a range of AI techniques to educational data that we have carefully prepared. The aim of this part of the AI Readiness process is to help you to "get under the skin" of the challenge that you face and understand how best to address this challenge. Including how to use AI tools, products, and services to help you address the challenge.

We hope you will have a much better idea about the sorts of roles that AI and human expertise can play and can continue to think about how they can work together most effectively. We also hope that you are starting to understand more about the potential value of an AI for you personally and for your colleagues.

Well done! You have now explored Step 6 of the AI Readiness programme. Chapter 7 will discuss the seventh and final step.

In this book, we can only scratch the surface of what is possible when it comes to AI and education, but scratching the surface is exactly what we must continue to do if we are to develop the best possible mapping of AI to the needs of students and teachers. So, keep scratching away!

USEFUL RESOURCES

http://www.pelars.eu
https://www.youtube.com/watch?v=CPqHB_34LRY
https://www.youtube.com/watch?v=qYfL-eitRNU
https://www.youtube.com/watch?v=klxxYrnrZyQ

NOTE

1 Cukurova, M., Luckin, R., & Kent, C. (2020). Impact of an artificial intelligence research frame on the perceived credibility of educational research

evidence. *International Journal of Artificial Intelligence in Education*, 30(2), 205–235. doi:10.1007/s40593-019-00188-w

Spikol, D., Ruffaldi, E., Dabisias, G., & Cukurova, M. (2018). Supervised machine learning in multimodal learning analytics for estimating success in project-based learning. *Journal of Computer Assisted Learning*, 34(4), 366–377. doi:10.1111/jcal.12263

Cukurova, M., Luckin, R., Millán, E., & Mavrikis, M. (2018). The NISPI framework: Analysing collaborative problem-solving from students' physical interactions. *Computers and Education*, 116, 93–109. doi:10.1016/j. compedu.2017.08.007

7

ETHICAL QUESTIONS
AND WHAT IS NEXT?

Each chapter in this book has shown you one of the steps in the AI Readiness Framework. Each chapter takes you a step towards being ready to make the most of AI. Everyone can be AI Ready and everyone should be AI ready. Once you are AI ready you will understand where AI can best be applied and why AI is the right tool for the job. You will also understand more about the implications that AI brings for teachers, learners, and parents.

In this closing chapter, we will explain what Step 7 in the AI Readiness Framework is all about, and we will explore some of the ethical challenges and questions that AI's use in education produces. We will also discuss what you might do next to continue learning about AI and how the understanding that we hope this book has helped you to develop can be applied when looking at some of the AI products and services that are currently available to you.

THE ETHICS OF AI FOR
TEACHING AND LEARNING

Throughout this book, we have regularly alerted you to ethical issues as they have arisen, chapter by chapter. Ethical AI is essential when it comes to education; it must always be at the centre of any development and decision-making concerning AI and its use in education.

DOI: 10.1201/9781003193173-7

The AI Readiness Framework that underpins the structure of this book and that we described in our introduction has the acronym EThICAL, quite deliberately to ensure that ethics is always front of mind. But how can you as a teacher or headteacher play your role ethically when buying and applying AI?

This question was a focal point for the Institute of Ethical AI in Education (IEAIED)[1] that worked internationally to consult and collate views from multiple educational stakeholders to produce a four-page framework designed for education.[2] The express purpose of the framework is to guide those who are selecting and buying, or thinking of buying, AI for their school, so that they know the right questions to ask and actions to take. Please use the framework to help you make decisions that are right for your school.

As an example of how the framework can help you, here are the nine objectives that the IEAIED recommend that you adopt when considering the use of AI:

1 **Achieving educational goals**. AI should be used to achieve well-defined educational goals based on strong societal, educational, or scientific evidence that this is for the benefit of the learner.

2 **Forms of assessment**. AI should be used to assess and recognise a broader range of learners' talents.

3 **Administration and workload**. AI should increase the capacity of organisations whilst respecting human relationships.

4 **Equity**. AI systems should be used in ways that promote equity between different groups of learners and not in ways that discriminate against any group of learners.

5   **Autonomy**. AI systems should be used to increase the level of control that learners have over their learning and development.

6 **Privacy**. A balance should be struck between privacy and the legitimate use of data for achieving well-defined and desirable educational goals.

7   **Transparency and accountability**. Humans are ultimately responsible for educational outcomes and should therefore have an appropriate level of oversight of how AI systems operate.

8 **Informed participation**. Learners, educators, and other relevant practitioners should have a reasonable understanding of AI and its implications.

9 **Ethical design**. AI resources should be designed by people who understand the impacts these resources will have.

Each of these objectives has a set of criteria and a set of associated questions for you to ask yourself, your colleagues, and the company wanting to sell you their AI. For example, Objective 1, "achieving educational goals", has the following eight associated questions. The text in brackets indicates the point in time at which the question is appropriate:

1 Have you clearly identified the educational goal that is to be achieved through the use of AI? (*Pre-procurement*)

2 Can you explain why a particular AI resource has the capacity to achieve the educational goal specified above? (*Pre-procurement*)

3 What impact do you expect to achieve through the use of AI, and how will you measure and assess this impact? (*Pre-procurement*)

4 What information have you received from the suppliers, and are you satisfied that the AI resource is capable of achieving your desired objectives and impacts? (*Procurement*)

5 What information have you received from the suppliers, and are you satisfied that measures of student performance are aligned with recognised and accepted test instruments and/ or measures that are based on societal, educational, or scientific evidence? (*Procurement*)

6 How will you monitor and assess the extent to which the intended impacts and objectives are being achieved? (*Monitoring and evaluation*)

7 Can the supplier confirm that periodic reviews are conducted and that these reviews verify that the AI resource is effective and performing as intended? (*Monitoring and evaluation*)

8 If the impacts of using AI as intended were not satisfactory, why was this the case? What steps will you take in order to achieve improved impacts? (*Monitoring and evaluation*)

ARE YOU AI READY?

There are seven steps in the AI Readiness Programme and each of the chapters in this book has explained the learning involved in one of these steps. The seventh step is both the end and the beginning. The seventh step is: Iterate. What does this mean? Firstly, it means that we want you to keep learning. To repeat each of the steps from one to six as many times as you need to for you to be confident in your AI Readiness. Secondly, it indicates that AI Readiness is an ongoing endeavour.

We can always learn more about the problems and challenges that we face as teachers by exploring the relevant data, applying AI thinking and AI tools and techniques too. Once you see the problems and challenges that you face with an AI mindset, then you will be able to make better decisions about how these problems and challenges can be addressed. You will also know if there is a possible role for AI in the way these challenges should be addressed.

When I, Rose, studied AI at university, it was a subject that was fundamentally about solving problems intelligently. I now worry that this particular aspect of AI has become somewhat overshadowed by the hype around deep learning AI[3] and how it is going to revolutionise everything. And yet, it is the problem-solving aspect of AI that is still the most important.

For example, you are worried about the huge marking workload that you and your colleagues are dealing with. On the face of things, this looks like a problem about the process of marking, and it may well be. However, it may also be a problem that is about something else completely, such as:

- The type of activities and assessments that pupils are being asked to complete. Are too many of them producing outputs that require a teacher to mark them? Could some of these activities be redesigned to allow self-marking or peer marking?

- Is the problem as much about the time it takes teachers to construct appropriate feedback for students, as it is about calculating exactly what mark the pupil should be allocated?
- Or is the problem about being able to explain, evidence, and justify to pupils and parents why you, the teacher, are suggesting that a particular set of revised learning goals should be put in place?

These questions only scratch the surface of the questions that must be asked if you are really going to understand the precise nature of the problem at the heart of the teacher time challenge.

Unless you do take your time to probe, prod, deconstruct, and scrutinise the problem, it will be all too easy for you to be persuaded that an AI product that automatically does the marking for teachers is the solution. AI is extremely accurate and fast. It uses absolutely the latest and most sophisticated deep learning AI to produce its marks. However, if the real problem is about the quality of feedback that pupils require, then an AI marking product is not going to help you. Similarly, if the real problem concerns the types of activities and assessments that pupils are required to complete, then the AI marker is not going to crack your problem either. And if the real cause of the problem lies in the need for them to be able to explain and justify their decisions, then forget the AI marker, no matter how fast and accurate it is, it will not be able to help you when it comes to justifying and explaining the marks it has allocated, let alone why they support a decision to revise learning goals.

The point here is that you must unpack all the assumptions that are part of the challenge or problem you want to solve. You must understand the precise nature of the challenge or problem if you are really going to reach a solution. Data and AI are "your friends" as you unfold the layers and unpack the nuances of your challenges. So, go on, use the AI Readiness 7-Step approach to get intimate with your data, cosy up to your assumptions, and "make friends with AI". You will reap the benefits for a long time to come.

SO HOW CAN YOUR NEW KNOWLEDGE HELP YOU UNDERSTAND THE EDUCATIONAL AI PRODUCTS THAT ARE OUT THERE?

You may be wondering how your new-found understanding of AI is going to help you understand more about the sorts of educational AI products that are available. We are therefore going to look at some of these products and explain the connection between your AI Readiness and the way that these systems use AI.

The number of AI products and services designed for K–12 education is growing and it is impossible for us to explain all of them. However, we will cover the following categories of AI products and services for schools and you can find links to examples for each category at the end of the chapter.

AI ADAPTIVE TUTORING SOFTWARE

We discussed adaptivity, as one of the key characteristics of AI in Chapter 1, when we introduced you to the distinct types of AI, from GOFAI to modern machine learning AI. Not surprisingly, the fact that AI can behave in an adaptive manner is especially useful in education. One of the ways in which AI's ability to adapt is applied to education is in the creation of adaptive tutoring software. This AI adapts to the needs of an individual pupil, or tutee, to provide a teaching session that is unique to that pupil.

However, whilst adaptivity is the general aim of all AI adaptive tutoring software, not all tutoring software adapts in the same way. Software may differ in their pedagogical approach. For example, an adaptive tutoring product might adopt a behaviourist pedagogy and vary the complexity of the content and the activities that each pupil is asked to complete, but not adapt the order in which topics and activities are presented. The data that drives the decision by the AI to adapt an activity or content is driven purely by each learner's performance in the activities and assessments they complete. The feedback and support provided by the software is minimal and plays no part in the software's decision-making process.

Alternatively, the pedagogy of an AI adaptive tutoring product might be more constructivist. In this case, the emphasis on the adaptivity may be placed on providing the most appropriate sort of support to each pupil to help them construct their own understanding. There may be few changes to the content or sequence of tasks, but differentiation of the activities and assessments, and a great deal of adaptivity to the feedback is provided to the pupil by the software. The activities each learner receives are also made simpler or more complex. This type of decision made by the AI about what and when to adapt is based upon the way the pupil uses the support provided by the software to complete activities successfully. These are just two examples of how AI adaptive tutoring software can be quite different.

AI adaptive tutoring software can vary in more ways than the pedagogical approach that it uses, but pedagogy is what differentiates the two AI adaptive tutoring software products Mathia[4] and Enskills.[5]

The pedagogy at the heart of Mathia is called *model tracing* and it stems from early work completed by John Anderson (we mentioned him in Chapter 1) with production rules and GOFAI. An expert mathematician would provide a model of the steps that needed to be taken to solve every math problem encompassed by the software, including all the possible erroneous steps that a pupil might take. When a pupil used the software, their actions would be traced back to the expert's model to find out how the tutoring software should progress the pupil. The modern Mathia product has evolved and uses a mix of machine learning and rules-based AI, but the basic principles of model tracing remain.

Enskills, on the other hand, is based on early work done by its founder Lewis Johnson, who speaks many languages himself and believes that language learning must be culturally contextualized. The systems that his company Alelo develops therefore stress the cultural authenticity of the language learning activities a pupil completes. The Enskills software operates via a web browser and each pupil can speak to an on-screen character, who will respond.

The response given by the onscreen character is adapted according to what the pupil has said, how correct their grammar and pronunciation is, and how much progress is being made.

All the activities the pupil completes are adapted and contextual in meaningful settings and language. Enskills uses natural language processing and speech recognition and interpretation AI as well as adaptivity. It is therefore a good example of AI adaptive tutoring software that uses AI for multiple different purposes: to adapt to the pupil, to interpret what the pupil has said, and to produce a spoken response. It probably will not surprise you to know that Enskills uses a variety of applications of machine learning to behave intelligently.

ADAPTIVE PLATFORMS THAT USE AI

Beyond adaptive software tutors that focus on a particular subject area, there are also AI adaptive platforms that cover many areas of the curriculum and that can therefore enable teachers and pupils to compare their performances, misconceptions, behaviours, and needs across and between different subjects. An example of an AI adaptive platform is CENTURY Tech.[6] CENTURY combines Artificial Intelligence, neuroscience, and learning science into its technology to try to understand exactly what each learner needs in order to thrive and fill in the gaps in their knowledge. CENTURY uses spaced learning, interleaving and cognitive load theory, and learning from neuroscience research to help pupils embed knowledge in their long-term memory.

What is particularly interesting about CENTURY is that it is one of the few AI systems within education that uses deep machine learning to enable its AI to continually learn how each student learns, so that the CENTURY platform can adapt to their strengths and weaknesses to provide the support or challenge each student requires. Their founder, Priya Lakhani, described it to me like this:

> The key component of this process is a neural network[7] that, given a pair of student and question, predicts the expected level

of challenge that such student would experience if tested on that question.

AI RECOMMENDER SYSTEMS

Sometimes, rather than actually teaching or tutoring, AI is used to help you find the most appropriate resources for yourself to learn something new, or to help you find the best resource for your pupils, or to recommend a learning pathway to them. For example, Adaptemy[8] is a company that helps organisations, including schools, add adaptivity to their existing content or learning platform. The Adaptemy "AI engine" provides each learner with a recommendation about which concept to learn next based on the ability of the student, which concepts they have worked on, the positions of the concepts in the course map, and the student's motivation. There is also the opportunity for teachers to input to the recommendation system, even overwriting it if that is what they believe is best for the student. There are some interesting research papers on the company website if you would like to know more.[9]

Similarly, Area9 Lyceum provides adaptivity for existing resources. Originally developed for the corporate training market, there is now a K–12 option available.[10] In addition, Bibblio, whilst not a tool solely for teachers, is an AI-driven content recommendation system that could be used in education and their website contains a nice explanation about how AI is used in their software.[11]

COMPANIES CAN BE COY

It is often hard to find out exactly what kind of AI a company is using to power their product; they don't like to give the game away to their competitors. However, we think they could be more transparent without letting the AI out of the bag. It is always possible that the AI that they describe is not much AI at all. However, with your new-found AI Readiness and the IEAIED question guidelines, be confident and probe the companies that want to sell you their wares.

LAST WORDS

We told you in the introduction that we want you to see how AI can help you, and we want you to understand how to work alongside AI, so that AI empowers you. We want you to feel confident buying AI so that it will be useful and appropriate for you. But, remember, most of all we want you to realise how amazing *you* are, because the correct role for AI is to make you, your colleagues, your team, and your students the smartest, most effective people you can be.

Make a friend in AI and enjoy where that takes you.

USEFUL RESOURCES

EdSurge (2016). *Decoding adaptive*. London: Pearson.
https://www.pearson.com/content/dam/one-dot-com/one-dot-com/uk/documents/educator/primary/Pearson-Decoding-Adaptive-Report.pdf

NOTES

1 https://www.buckingham.ac.uk/research-the-institute-for-ethical-ai-in-education/
2 https://fb77c667c4d6e21c1e06.b-cdn.net/wp-content/uploads/2021/03/The-Institute-for-Ethical-AI-in-Education-The-Ethical-Framework-for-AI-in-Education.pdf
3 https://en.wikipedia.org/wiki/Deep_learning AND https://www.deeplearning.ai
4 https://www.carnegielearning.com/solutions/math/mathia/
5 https://www.alelo.com/english-language-teaching/
6 https://www.century.tech
7 A neural network is a form of machine learning that is used by deep learning systems. You can find out more about neural networks here: https://towardsdatascience.com/introducing-deep-learning-and-neural-networks

-deep-learning-for-rookies-1-bd68f9cf5883 AND https://www.dee-plearning.ai

8 https://www.adaptemy.com/engine/
9 https://www.adaptemy.com/effective-learning-recommendations-pow-ered-by-ai-engine/
10 https://area9lyceum.com/k-12-education/
11 https://www.bibblio.org/tech

INDEX

Printed in the United States
by Baker & Taylor Publisher Services